MAR
COS

GRANADA

with Local Tips
The author's special recommendations are highlighted in yellow throughout this guide

There are six symbols to help you find your way around this guide:

Marco Polo's top recommendations

sites with a great view

where the local people meet

where young people get together

(A1)
map references

follow this route on the map for the best sights in the Costa del Sol

MARCO ⊕ POLO

Other travel guides and language guides in this series:

Algarve • Amsterdam • Australia • Brittany • California
Costa Brava/Barcelona • Côte d'Azur • Crete • Cuba • Cyprus
Florence • Florida • Gran Canaria • Greek Islands • Ireland • Istanbul
Mallorca • Malta • New York • New Zealand • Normandy
Paris • Prague • Rhodes • Rome • South Africa
Tenerife • Turkish Coast • Tuscany • Venice

French • German • Italian • Spanish

*Marco Polo would be very interested to hear your
comments and suggestions. Please write to:*

*World Leisure Marketing Ltd
Marco Polo Guides
9 Downing Road, West Meadows
Derby DE21 6HA England*

*Cover photograph: Cala Honda in Nerja (Schapowalow/Thiele)
Photographs: Irek (22, 37, 45); Janicke (28); Jung (16, 21, 64); Kallabis (inside cover, 12, 41, 76);
Lade: Welsh (80); Mauritius: Krautwurst (47), Rossenbach (57), Thonig (48, 52, 58, 67);
Strobel (4, 6, 9, 26, 34, 60, 68, 69, 86); Trummer (18, 24, 92)*

*1st English edition 1998
© Mairs Geographischer Verlag, Ostfildern Germany
Author: Roland Mischke
Translation: Alison Layland
English edition: Cathy Muscat, Emma Kay
Editorial director: Ferdinand Ranft
Design and layout: Thienhaus/Wipperman
Printed in Italy*

CONTENTS

Discover the Costa del Sol

*An enticing combination of deserted high Sierras
and thronging beach resorts*

When evening falls over the gardens of the Generalife, the Alhambra palace glows like a jewel in the dusk. The wind rustles through the oak and cypress trees, the fountains gurgle softly, and dappled shadows creep across the intricately patterned walls that reflect the creative mastery of the long-departed Moorish rulers. Within these ancient walls, time seems to have stood still. The reddish stone of the Alcazaba, the oldest part of the great palace, changes hue with the changing light. From dawn until dusk, its walls seem to soak up the sunlight, reflecting it back out at the end of the day to the darkening world around. For a while after the sun has gone down, you can still make out the symmetrical gardens around the palace where roses, palms, laurels and dark-green lakes stand out against the spectacular backdrop of the Sierra Nevada. The gates and patios, the weathered brickwork

of the sturdy defensive walls, the delicate, almost excessive, refinement of the ornamented passages and halls of the palaces, are bathed in this soft light until the pitch black of night finally sets in, shrouding their magnificence until the dawn breaks.

In southern Spain, every tree, every stone, every hill and every bend in the road conceals traces of a glorious past. The awesome palaces and monuments scattered across the landscape bear witness to a vanished oriental civilization. You can feel the weight of centuries of history, centred around the three great cities of Cordoba, Seville and, of course, Granada.

'Give him alms, woman, for there is nothing in life so cruel as to be blind in Granada'. This plea is inscribed on a ceramic plaque on one of the Alhambra walls. The setting of the legendary city in the east of Andalusia is quite dramatic, as it nestles between two foothills of the Sierra Nevada, with the blue-green mountains rising up behind it, and a fertile green plain stretching out to the west. The city itself boasts a wealth of fine architecture and

The Spanish 'caballero' and his gypsy daughter – it may look like a cliché, but old traditions die hard

The Sierra Nevada provides a fitting backdrop for the equally majestic Alhambra palace

the treasures of a great past, and has been designated a World Heritage Site by UNESCO. These hills have been a meeting point for different races and cultures for centuries. The area has been inhabited since the 5th century, but remained sparsely populated until the 13th century, as neither the Romans, Visigoths, nor any other settlers, attempted to urbanize it. All this changed with the rise of the Nasrids, an Islamic dynasty founded in 1238, which withstood the advances of the Christian *Reconquista* (reconquest) until 1492, and, during its two-and-a-half centuries of rule, brought the extent of Islamic culture and influence in Spain to a high point, the like of which has never been seen since.

It was during this time that the Alhambra was built as the royal seat of the Moorish rulers of Granada. The name Granada is, in fact, derived from the Moorish word *karnattah*, not from the Spanish *granada* (pomegranate) as many believe, though the fruit

does feature on the city's coat of arms. It took the armies of the Catholic monarchs Ferdinand and Isabella ten hard years of fighting before the last Moorish bastion on the Iberian peninsula fell to Christianity, and the hold of Islam over this part of Europe was finally broken. The handover of the city took place peacefully, without pillage or looting, as the last Nasrid ruler, Boabdil, was wise enough to come to a negotiated agreement with the Catholic monarchs, who allowed him safe passage out of the country after he capitulated to them. The victorious Catholics were thus able to enter and take possession of a beautiful city, with its rich architectural legacy intact.

The most architecturally impressive buildings in Andalusia date from the Moorish period, and the overall culture of the region is infused with Arab influences. Many of the caliphs were highly educated, and liked to gather academics and writers around them, enjoying their lively and learned discussions. The benefits of the long period of Moorish rule extended to the whole of Spain: Christians from the non-Moorish parts of the country sent their sons to be educated in the Arabic south, and the arts and sciences flourished. Muslims, Jews and Christians lived in close proximity to one another, and the region was renowned throughout Europe for its racial and religious tolerance. Then came the *Reconquista*, which brought with it discrimination and religious fanaticism, putting an end to a unique and flourishing culture.

This period of Moorish rule is now regarded as a 'Golden Age' in Spain's history. Granada's community was multicultural, with Jewish doctors, diplomats and philosophers among its leading figures (the city was often referred to as the 'City of the Jews'). At the same time, the Islamic rulers succeeded in maintaining an amicable relationship with the Christian Castilians. Building and architectural design were at their peak, and the exceedingly liberal spirit of the age gave the necessary freedom for medicine, sculpture, painting, poetry, music and dance to flourish. The population of Granada at the height of Arab rule was around 200 000, four times the population of London at that time.

Although Granada may not have witnessed such a thriving period since its heyday in the Middle Ages, the influences of this era can still be felt today. Franco's fascism never really took hold here. The people of Granada are still known for their open-mindedness and liberal attitudes,

and the population is predominantly young. This youthful, innovative spirit combined with a deeply rooted sense of history is what makes Granada such a fascinating place to visit.

The Costa del Sol beach resorts provide a total change of scene and require a different approach. Take Torremolinos. The traffic-free Calle San Miguel, lined with luxurious houses, restaurants and boutiques, forms the heart of the town, and cuts through the mass of grotesque concrete hotel blocks which tower over what was once a small romantic fishing village. At fiesta time the whole pedestrian area is filled with dancers, young women in brightly-coloured, ruched dresses with plunging necklines, and young men in tight-fitting trousers, short, embroidered jackets and broad-brimmed hats. The women move gracefully over the paving stones while the men strut and weave in and out among them – the stamping of boots, clicking of castanets, swirling of skirts, and the flashing of eyes can be seen and heard all around. The air is filled with exuberance, flirtatiousness and *joie de vivre* and the cares of everyday life are forgotten. This is the hedonistic Costa del Sol, 'the Sunny Coast', of the holiday brochures.

As with so many other once-idyllic places in southern Europe, the tourist boom of the 1960s and 1970s spoilt much of Spain's picturesque coastline. Concrete developments sprang up all along the coast to accommodate the huge numbers of package tourists flying in from northern European countries, and were allowed to spread unchecked.

Places like Torremolinos and Fuengirola were swamped in hurriedly-built hotels. The view of Torremolinos from the sea was transformed into a 10-km wall of concrete rising up behind the bleached straw of thousands of parasols, covering the Playa del Saltillo in the west right across to the Playa de los Álamos in the east. The sea became more and more polluted, the beaches dirty, and the sheer volume of people and noise made for a less than relaxing holiday. The rising crime rate put the finishing touches to the increasingly shabby image of the Costa del Sol. In the 1980s, holidaymakers, now more discerning in terms of quality and environment, stayed away in increasing numbers, and the Costa del Sol became yesterday's news as a holiday resort.

The concrete carbuncles are still there, but the owners of the high-rise blocks, apartment complexes and giant hotels have learnt a great deal from the uncontrolled frenzy of development that took place during the boom years. Extensive remodelling of existing buildings and judiciously-designed new structures have given the area a more welcoming appearance, flowers are being cultivated on the balconies, and the lush green leaves of climbing plants are helping to cover up 15-storey high concrete façades. The dubious alliances of politicians, developers, financiers, property sharks and creative accountants have been disbanded, and the beaches have now been cleaned up to such an extent that the EU is repeatedly awarding environmental commendations to the Costa del Sol.

Whole teams are sent in to tidy up parks and promenades, and trees are being planted in vast numbers. Tourist police in snow-white uniforms patrol the beaches and towns on foot or on horseback to ensure personal safety. A well-designed network of ring roads and motorways keeps the worst of the traffic well away from many of the built-up areas along the coast. Nature reserves have been designated across the region, so that now 18% of the 87 000 sq km of Andalusia benefits from some form of environmental protection.

The image of miles of concrete *urbanizaciones*, unimaginative holiday complexes and bungalow estates automatically conjured up by the words 'Costa del Sol' is a hard one to dislodge, yet the objective traveller will find quite a few undisturbed corners and hidden treasures here. Even Torremolinos, with its reputation for concrete and lager louts, now boasts beautifully-planted terraces which are a haven for songbirds, passages just wide enough for one person to squeeze through, where flowers in tubs cascade through balcony railings, street names prettily painted on to ceramic tiles fixed to whitewashed walls, shady courtyards behind magnificent wrought-iron gates, residential streets where the faint sound of guitar music can be heard and where the air is filled with the smells of Andalusian cooking and the heady scent of jasmine.

Sleek white yachts can once more be seen sailing up and down the sea in front of that former playground of the rich and famous, Marbella. Until recently this city, with its bold architecture and wonderful surroundings, where mountains and sea both boast a warm and pleasant climate, was known as the 'Costa del Crime'. This was where film and television stars, pop stars and influential businessmen rubbed shoulders with shady dealers, petty criminals, notorious politicians and the jet set. All this has changed. Marbella has sobered up. Though much of the concrete jungle remains, it is still a magnet for the rich and famous, but the money that circulates here nowadays is far less likely to have been stolen or laundered!

The same holds true for the rest of the coast. The snobbery of the past seems to have waned, making way for a new refreshingly unpretentious attitude. The Costa del Sol is no longer the favourite haunt of playboys, ageing rock stars and their groupies, but that of a new wave of tourists who come here with a sincere interest in discovering the area's native traditions, for this is a land, despite all the development and mass tourism of recent years, that still boasts a deeply-rooted ancient culture.

The first settlers came to the southern coast of Spain in the Palaeolithic era, more than 22 000 years ago. Cave tombs, skeletons and sacred sites all bear witness to a thriving prehistoric culture. They were followed by Phoenicians, Greeks and Carthaginians, Romans, Visigoths and other peoples, all of whom left traces of their presence. After the victory of the Christians over the Moors, who had dominated the Iberian peninsula for nearly 800 years (711-1492), Andalusia prof-ited for a while from the discovery of the New World by Columbus, which gave Spain its prestigious status as the most powerful nation in the world. Thereafter the region gradually fell into decline and suffered poverty and hardship.

It is one of the remarkable facts of history that Andalusia was then forgotten for centuries, a backwater of little importance to the rest of Europe, despite the fact that it had once been the centre of a highly sophisticated civilization which bred so much culture. Once the base from which explorers set out to conquer the world, this land of smallholders and day labourers, marked by intense heat and incredible beauty, became a place with a glittering past but seemingly no future.

The narrowest of whitewashed alleyways are draped in flowers

It was not until this century that Andalusia was, in a sense, reconnected to the outside world as a result of the boom in tourism. The rush of tourists to the beaches has calmed down in recent years, as attitudes to tourism are changing. The inland regions are gaining in popularity. In the mountainous hinterland nature is flourishing unrestrained. Here an incredible variety of European and African flora and fauna abound: it is home to lynxes, the breeding ground of golden eagles, a perfect resting place for thousands of migratory birds, provides pastureland for semi-wild horses and a safe habitat for masses of storks and flamingos. The hills of the Sierras are dotted with white-washed villages, that shimmer in the intense sun like fields of snow. Between the sea and the inland mountain ranges which reach up to around 3400 m at their highest point, the varied landscape is truly breathtaking. Terrifying hairpin bends lead up into wild, romantic mountains with rocky outcrops sticking up like oversized, sun-bleached bones. Dried-up river beds full of pebbles and boulders wend their way between bare, red rocks. When the sunflowers are in bloom, hundreds of fields are transformed into spectacular oceans of yellow; and the olive plantations stretch out to the horizon. The olive tree is one of the most enduring symbols of this region. Even though everything around it has changed, the olive tree remains unaltered by the effects of time, a constant landmark seen by all visitors to the region since the Stone Age.

When it comes to romantic scenery, the rugged hinterland has the edge over the coast. Away from the hustle and bustle of the resorts, peace reigns and the air is scented with thyme and roses. As you wend your way through the uplands and valleys you will stumble across many hidden treasures: small squares overgrown with orange trees; churches as big as cathedrals (so massive that their architects were considered to be slightly mad); cool bodegas where the fino sherry is drawn straight from barrels decorated with coats of arms. Little villages perch like eyries on the mountainsides. In these tiny settlements the idyllic atmosphere is created through sheer simplicity: a church, a village square, a small bakery, a scattering of white-washed houses, old women dressed in black seated in doorways, wizened old men sipping brandy and watching the world go by, playful children breaking the silence with their screams.

The perfect place to stop for a rest is in the local bar. The scene does not differ much from one village bar to the next. The floor will be covered with sawdust and there will be a television flickering in the corner. As you enter, the locals will stop their conversation, look at you for a while, then resume it, smiling. You might order a cool glass of honey-coloured wine made from the local Palomino grape. The owner will probably bring it over to you with a little plate of olives, and perhaps a few *calamares* or some oily *manchego* cheese. Sit back, enjoy the peace and quiet away from the coast, and soak up the history around you.

History at a glance

Prehistory
The first inhabitants of the Costa del Sol were Palaeolithic nomads who settled here around 20 000 years ago

c. 1000 BC
Phoenician merchants from the eastern Mediterranean settle in the region and establish the port of Cadiz

800 until 300 BC
First the Greeks, then the Carthaginians, establish trading posts in southern Spain

From 218 BC
The Romans take control of the Iberian peninsula

1st BC-3rd century AD
The peaceful development of the coastal region encourages trade and prosperity

From 4 AD
The fall of the Roman Empire. Rule of the peninsula is disputed between various Germanic tribes

711
The Arabs conquer southern Spain and name it al-Andalus

8th-11th century
Economic and cultural life flourishes under Islamic rule

Mid-11th-15th century
The state disintegrates into small Islamic kingdoms, ruled over by taifas. Christian armies penetrate further and further into Andalusia, which eventually falls to Castile – except for the kingdom of Granada

1492
The Christian Reconquest of Spain is finally completed as the Nasrid dynasty capitulates to the Catholic Monarchs Ferdinand V of Aragon and Isabella I of Castile

From 1609
Jews and as many as half a million Muslims converted to Christianity are driven out

1704
Spanish war of succession. The English take Gibraltar

End of the 19th century
Economic decline as the Spanish colonies are lost

1931
Spain becomes a Republic, and the king leaves the country

1936-39
Following the electoral victory of the left-wing Popular Front, Franco invades Andalusia with the Army of Africa from Morocco. The Spanish Civil War leaves over half a million dead

From 1960
The Costa del Sol becomes the most popular tourist destination in southern Europe

1975
Death of Franco; King Juan Carlos becomes head of state

1981
Andalusia becomes an autonomous province

1986
Spain enters the EU

Customs and culture

Aspects of Andalusian life, past and present

Bullfighting

La Corrida de toros, perhaps the most emblematic of Spain's national traits, has a very special place in Andalusian folklore. The majority of staunch bullfighting aficionados hail from the region, as do the most famous *matadores* (killers). Andalusians confidently assert that they alone appreciate the true beauty of the *tauromaquía*, an allusion to the metaphysical dimension of the fight in which death is always present: the confrontation between man and beast in strictly regulated conditions corresponds to the belief that people need to view life and death as fate and as a unified whole.

While it may be possible to justify bullfighting in philosophical terms, for most outsiders it is still a bloodthirsty and cruel sport. However, animal rights activists are not always aware of the grave ecological consequences its abolition would have. In Hemingway's words, 'The fighting bull is as far removed from the domesticated bull as a wolf is from a dog'.

Flamenco, the soul of Andalusia

The *toros bravos* are from a unique breed of cattle which would die out without the existence of the bullfight. Until the moment of their death in the arena, they graze in pastures which are the habitat of rare forms of plant and animal life; these would become extinct without the bulls, as the pastureland would soon be transformed into intensive farming land. Nor can the economic importance of the breeding of the fighting bulls and the *corrida* itself be ignored, as thousands of Andalusians make their living from the sport.

Bullfights are held from Easter to October, every Sunday in the larger towns. In recent years, the spectacle has become increasingly popular with the young, and although enjoyment of the *corrida* may once have been reserved for the macho Andalusian male, more women than men now flock to the *fiesta nacional*. In order to appreciate the bullfight for what it is, a basic understanding of the sequence of events is essential: the *paseo*, the entrance procession of the participants, is followed by the bringing in of

13

two bulls to be fought by three *matadores*. The *banderilleros*, with their short, barbed darts, and the *picadores* on horseback, with their lances, work the bull up into a frenzy. In the *tercio de la muerte* (the third part in which the killing takes place), the *matador* comes in with his *muleta*, the red cape. Having weakened the bull with deft manoeuvres, he attempts the *estocada*, the fatal sword thrust. Through the precise moves of his *muleta* he encourages the bull to lower its head, so that he can thrust his sword between its shoulder blades. If his aim is true, the sword should penetrate directly to the heart whereupon the bull's death is instantaneous. If he is less competent, he is ridiculed by the audience, and the beast is given the *descabello*, the coup de grace, with the dagger. The *matador* is awarded one ear, both ears or even the two ears and the tail of the bull, depending on his performance. The latter is the highest form of recognition of his art.

Feria

The Andalusians love festivals, and throw themselves wholeheartedly into all kinds of celebrations. Over 3000 different *ferias*, pilgrimages, carnivals, Islamic festivals and Christian processions take place throughout the year across Andalusia. Most of the larger villages and towns have their own *feria* (which literally means fair or market), which is usually held during the week of celebrations surrounding their patron saint's day. It is a reflection of the region's way of life, combining religious celebration with *joie de vivre*, local pride and pure exuberance.

Flamenco

The world-famous Andalusian dance, accompanied by its distinctive singing and guitar music, arose from the *cante jondo*, one of the oldest forms of song. It has many forms, popular versions being *sevillanas* and *fandangos*, while in the coastal region *granadinas* and *malagueñas* predominate; surprisingly, none of these are 'true' flamenco in the strictest sense. The allure of flamenco lies in improvisation, not in the carefully choreographed performances laid on largely for the benefit of the tourists. When the dancers work themselves up to the greatest passion, Andalusians consider them to be possessed by the *duende* (demon). The genuine dance is a passionate representation of the extremes of emotion, ranging from joy to despair. While tourists tend to be drawn by the swirling of colourful skirts, the clicking of the castanets (which actually have no place in true flamenco) and the clapping of hands, the locals focus their attention on the quality of the singing and the graceful arm movements of the women.

Lifestyle

'O Spaniards, who will succeed in arousing you from your oppressive sleeping sickness?' raged Casanova as he travelled through Spain. He would not need to voice such a complaint today. Following the oppressive protectionism of Franco's regime, the Spanish resolutely embraced a free market economy. Spain's economic growth in recent years has been remarkable and has resulted in a whole new generation of companies and business people.

Commerce and hard work, which at one time would have been totally contrary to the honour of a *caballero*, whose traditional occupation was studied idleness, are now considered prerequisites for success. This change in attitude has deeply affected long-held Andalusian customs and lifestyles, and the new work ethic has brought with it a different way of life. Modern day Andalusia enjoys the same reputation it did in Moorish times – cosmopolitan and multilingual, tolerant and adaptable. The process of economic change which took place throughout Spain has been particularly exciting in the once traditional south, where time had stood still for so long.

That said, the Andalusian character hasn't completely changed. Even in the cut-throat commercial world, business is rarely done at great speed. The toughest negotiations are still conducted over long meals and couched in polite good manners. *'Genio y figura hasta la sepultura'* – 'Good behaviour and character from the cradle to the grave'. Unsurprisingly, this well-worn maxim still hangs on the walls of many an Andalusian house.

Mañana
This is one of those Spanish words which is frequently heard but not easy to translate. Its literal meaning is 'tomorrow', but as an expression it embodies far more than its literal sense. *Mañana*, with its implications of refusal, postponement, regret, and putting off until later, is not only a word but a philosophy, a way of life, a flexible principle. Put simply, *mañana* represents the Spanish temperament, a versatile expression which is not a brusque dismissal; rather it should be taken to mean: 'Tomorrow is another day'.

Neanderthals
On the basis of finds in caves near Málaga, some scientists have concluded that both Neanderthal and modern man lived alongside each other for around 10000 years. One of the current theories suggests that Neanderthals, like us, were descendants of the original Homo Sapiens, but developed in a different direction. Although their brains were as large as those of modern man, they had less imagination, especially when it came to the invention of tools and techniques. Some believe that modern man migrated to Europe from Africa around 40000 years ago, and eventually replaced Neanderthals, as their superior intelligence prevailed.

Paradores
There are just under a dozen *paradores* on the Costa del Sol, situated either inland or on the coast these are quality hotels in beautifully-restored palaces, castles, stately homes, country mansions or monasteries. They may be expensive, but a night spent in an upper-storey bedroom, with views over the surrounding countryside encompassing silvery rivers, golden wheat fields and mountain panoramas, is an incomparable and unforgettable experience. Most *paradores* were once in a state of decay; historical buildings whose owners did not have sufficient funds for their upkeep. The opportunity to preserve valuable structures from dereliction, while opening up an

especially interesting part of regional history to the public, was seized upon by the government which founded the state-owned range of top-class hotels. Most *paradores* have spacious, comfortable rooms and a delightfully typical Andalusian inner courtyard complete with bright flowers and a splashing fountain. Meals are often served beneath the vaulted ceiling of a refectory, at damask-covered tables laid with heavy silverware. Centuries of history emanate from the walls of these splendid hotels, the atmosphere of which is unique.

Religion

Spain is considered to be the most devoutly Roman Catholic country in the world, and of all Spaniards, none is more god-fearing than the Andalusian. Yet this piety is not overburdened with solemnity - quite the contrary. It is characterized by a real earthy passion. A religious festival without celebration, dancing and wine would be unimaginable in southern Spain. Pilgrimages and processions are by no means solemn events, not even during *Semana Santa* (Holy Week, before Easter). In Andalusia, religion is

characterized by freedom of choice. While God and the saints are revered and respected, they are also looked upon as old friends. This characteristically relaxed attitude to religion is wonderfully reflected in the book *The Spaniard and the Seven Deadly Sins.* The author, Fernando Díaz Plaja, provides his readers with a private telephone connection to God, through which deals are nonchalantly made: if the local football team wins, donations will be made to the poor; if a business deal is successful, the divorce will not go through; if the children pass their exams, the dog will never be kicked again. No Andalusian would consider such bribery as unethical; their relationship with God is a free and easy one. For all this, religion is taken seriously and is an integral part of everyday life.

Siesta

The afternoon siesta, which usually falls between 3 and 5 o'clock, is part and parcel of the relaxed rhythm of life in the south. It does take a while to get used to the fact that everything comes to a standstill at this time. Shops close and the streets empty, as

Málaga's arena as seen from the Gibralfaro castle

people take shelter in their cool indoor rooms and shaded courtyards from the fierce midday heat. But the daily rest is a custom that most holidaymakers would do well to adopt. It's the perfect opportunity to recover from your morning's exertions and recharge your batteries. You will wake up feeling refreshed and ready to continue well into the night in true Spanish style. People don't necessarily sleep during their siesta though. A recent survey has revealed that the majority of Spaniards are conceived at this time of day!

Water

The persistent drought in Andalusia means drinking water has to be rationed. The water supply on the Costa del Sol is regularly cut off, and in Granada residents often have to go without water for several hours a day. Visitors to the region should be careful therefore not only make allowances for the water shortages, but should also help out by using water sparingly.

Women

Barely two decades ago Spanish women were the least emancipated in the whole of Europe, powerless to do anything without the approval of their fathers, husbands or priests. They were not allowed to travel across the country without written permission, could not open a bank account, and in many cases could not even go for a walk without a chaperone, while the mere mention of contraception was taboo. As the women in the rest of Europe were progressing towards sexual equality, in Spain the deeply-rooted patriarchal society and power of the Catholic Church made sure that Spanish women remained more or less second-class citizens with few rights of their own. Courtships were heavily ritualized, pre-marital sex was regarded as a grievous sin, and engagement a binding duty.

This state of affairs changed radically after Franco's death, as Spanish women tried to catch up with their European counterparts at breakneck speed, with the backing of the new democracy. So much change after so many years of oppression was quite difficult to control, and the strong militant feminist movement that emerged after the death of the dictator was inevitable. Nowadays, however, the relationship between the sexes is more relaxed, and radical feminism has simmered down somewhat. Even in the south of Spain, women are now professionally active to a great extent and marriage is no longer viewed as such a rigid institution. The number of unmarried mothers is on the increase, while the birth rate has gone down significantly, as women from their teenage years have access to contraception.

Despite these social changes, most visitors to Spain will nevertheless be struck by the discrepancy that still exists between the role modern women play in society and the old-fashioned concept of womanhood. In Andalusia, more so than anywhere else in Spain, the basic traditional masculine and feminine roles have been preserved; the woman is desired and wooed, and the man is her strong protector.

The home of tapas

The portions may be bite-sized, but in Andalusia it's quality not quantity that counts

The inhabitants of the province of Granada and the Costa del Sol are thoroughly Andalusian when it comes to food. For Basques and Catalans, Galicians and Madrileños, eating is a serious, protracted affair; Andalusians do not feast, but prefer to nibble. They are not especially impressed with a copious table laden with sumptuous dishes, and go for quality rather than quantity. The best aspect of the region's cuisine is its simplicity.

Although tapas are served throughout Spain, the traditional bite-sized bar snacks originated in Andalusia and it is here that you will find them at their best. Literally translated, *tapa* means 'cover'. Originally, a glass of wine was served with a morsel of food on a small plate balanced on top of the glass: a piece of cheese, a few olives, a slice of sausage or ham. This custom gave rise to a whole culinary culture. Andalusians enjoy spending the evening

A ceiling hung with Serrano ham, the regional speciality from Trevélez in the Alpujarras

going from bar to bar, drinking a beer here, a glass of wine there, each accompanied by one or more tapas. The variety on offer is enormous. Here are a few of the more traditional tapas you may come across:

aceitunas – olives

albóndigas en salsa – meatballs in a spicy sauce

berenjenas – aubergines, often fried in batter

boquerones – fresh anchovies marinated in garlic and herbs

boquerones fritos – fresh fried anchovies

champiñones al ajillo – mushrooms fried in garlic

champiñones rellenos – stuffed mushrooms

chorizo – spicy red sausage

empanadillas de atún y aceitunas – small pastry cases with a tuna and olive filling

gambas al ajillo – prawns in garlic

jamon Serrano – cured ham

patatas (or papas) bravas – spicy potatoes, fried or baked

pinchitos con dátiles y ciruelas con bacon – dates and prunes on skewers wrapped in crispy bacon

pinchitos morunos – marinaded

pieces of meat on skewers

queso – cheese (the hard manchego is the most common)

tortilla – Spanish omelette (ie made with egg and potato)

Tapas can be eaten as appetizers, or else you can order a selection to make up a whole meal. They are often displayed in a glass case on the bar so that instead of having to struggle through your phrase book, all you need to do is point to the one you want to try next.

Alongside tapas, gazpacho is one of southern Spain's best-known culinary inventions. It is basically a cold soup made from ripe, juicy tomatoes, cucumber, green peppers, onions, soaked stale white bread, vinegar, olive oil and a great deal of garlic – all formerly leftovers from the tables of the nobility. The ingredients are puréed, seasoned with salt and pepper, and thinned down with water. The soup is then left to mature for one or two hours in the fridge. It is deliciously refreshing in the hot southern climate and is, in fact, the one dish specifically from Andalusia that is recognised in gourmet establishments all over the world.

Andalusian cuisine can in no way be called grandiose. In contrast to other Spanish provinces it prefers a degree of understatement. While Galicians, Catalans and, above all, Basques have produced a number of famous chefs, Andalusia has a reputation for being the *zona de los fritos*, 'the fried dish zone'. Although frying may be the most popular cooking method, the dishes are never over-greasy. They are lightly fried in olive oil, and usually based around fish and seafood. Meat is also served, of course, but it does not play a major role in Andalusian cuisine. This disappointed Ernest Hemingway, who observed: 'The Andalusians rear magnificent bulls, fight skilfully with them, put them to death in a breathtaking manner – but they do not know how to cook them'. There is one exception, however: *rabo de toro*, braised bull's tail, which is a regular feature on the southern Spanish menu, especially in Granada. Another local meat speciality is the exceptional *jamón serrano*. This ham comes from the pigs which roam freely through the great oak woods of the hinterland region. It is cured in the snows of the Sierra and dried in the wind. No true Andalusian can resist it.

On the whole, meat is either grilled or fried, and served with fried potatoes and a salad if you are lucky. Fish and seafood, on the other hand, come in all sorts of imaginative guises and there is a wide variety on offer – fresh tuna (*atún*); swordfish (*pez espada*); monkfish (*rape*); lobster (*langosta*); red mullet (*salmonete*) and skate (*raya*); prawns (*gambas*); king prawns (*langostinos*) and squid (*calamares*). Classic fish dishes include: *Sopa de pescado*, a thick fish soup; *pescado frito*, fish (usually cod or hake) fried to perfection; *zarzuela*, a fish and seafood stew; and, of course, *paella*, which, although it originates from Valencia, is a favourite dish across the country. The classic dish is made with saffron rice and a mixture of seafood, seafood and meat, or just meat.

The traditional Andalusian *tortilla* looks like a flan, and is made not just with potato but with all kinds of vegetables which can be grown in any garden. It is the seasoning, however, which gives this southern version its original taste.

Breakfast is best eaten in a bar or café rather than in your hotel. It is not a copious affair and usually consists of a milky coffee (*café con leche*) and a pastry (*pasta*) or bread roll/toast with jam (*panecillo/tostada con mermelada*). A more substantial alternative is the traditional *chocolate con churros*, a cup of very thick drinking chocolate served with deep-fried doughnut sticks that you dip into the chocolate. If you prefer something savoury, a slice of tortilla makes a nice change.

Mealtimes in Spain are late in comparison to northern Europe. Lunch is rarely eaten before 2 o'-clock, and the main meal of the day never begins before 9 o'clock, except in holiday resorts and restaurants catering predominantly for tourists. *La merienda* is an afternoon snack taken around 5 o'clock that fills the long gap between lunch and dinner. When looking for the right restaurant,

it's always best to make your decision spontaneously, letting the atmosphere of an establishment capture you and draw you in, rather than a dubious recommendation or price list. If you are unsure, it's best not to tie yourself down to one place by ordering a large meal – sample the wares first by trying a few tapas. If they are not to your taste, then go on to the next place you like the look of and start again.

Meals are invariably accompanied by local wines (*vino tinto*, red wine, or *vino blanco*, white wine). Andalusian wines are dominated by the world-famous sherry produced in the region – *Vino de Jerez*. It comes in a variety of forms, which can be divided into four categories: *fino* (dry, best served chilled), the nutty *amontillado* (medium dry), the deep golden *oloroso* (medium sweet) and *jerez dulce* (sweet cream sherry almost exclusively destined for export). The delicate flavour of the fine dry sherry makes it the perfect accompaniment to tapas.

Tapas and sherry: a simple but perfect combination

From tourist kitsch to genuine crafts

You'll need to shop around to find quality handmade goods among the mountains of cheap souvenirs

The artisanal traditions of Andalusia go back centuries. Many of the techniques and designs which are still used today are of Moorish origin. Granada is the best place to pick up handmade arts and crafts; ceramics are an especially good buy. The earthenware pots and crockery are original, colourful, and generally good value for money. The green and blue patterned jars and waterjugs are unmistakable, their designs often incorporating a pomegranate. Pottery from the village of Coín is also well worth considering. The pretty tiles you see for sale at roadside stalls make especially good mementoes.

Baskets made of esparto grass make unusual and practical souvenirs. You can pick them up in the villages of the Alpujarras, in Antequera, and a number of places along the coast. Sturdy and hard-wearing, they come in a variety of attractive designs and are especially good for market shopping.

Bazaar atmosphere at the Alcaicería in Granada

Look out for wrought iron and silver filigree artefacts and leather goods in the towns and villages of the hinterland. The leather goods are often handmade locally using traditional processes, and you will be hard pressed to find a mass-produced product that can compare in quality.

Mijas is a well-known centre for pretty embroidery, although a certain kitsch element creeps in to some of the items made for tourists.

All shops that display the 'Artespaña' sign are well worth a visit. These businesses are promoted by the government, and are scrupulous in their respect for the traditions of Andalusian arts and crafts; you can be sure you will not find 'Made in Taiwan' on any of the goods sold in these quality controlled outlets. If you are souvenir hunting anywhere else, be sure to shop around. The Costa del Sol is the land of souvenirs par excellence. Much of what you'll see is exorbitantly priced junk. As long as there is a market for kitsch souvenirs, there will always be someone who is happy to take cash for trash.

Processions and water pageants

*Boat parades, equestrian events, flamenco festivals –
something for everyone*

When it comes to celebrations and putting on a show, the Andalusians are expert. Every village in the province of Granada and the Costa del Sol has its own feast day. Not a day passes by without some kind of fiesta taking place somewhere in the region. The form these celebrations take has changed very little over the centuries. They are as wild and anarchic as they have always been. Characterized by their colour and exuberance they are often pagan in nature, based on rites which pre-date Christianity in Spain. The most important dates in the Andalusian festive calendar are determined by religious and secular criteria in equal measure. Málaga is known as the 'city of festivals', as it is the place which holds the most fiestas. For up-to-date information on festival listings telephone *(95) 24 81 12 51* (Málaga). The information is given out in several languages.

Semana Santa processions are held all over the Costa del Sol: a colourful spectacle to entertain even the most confirmed agnostic

PUBLIC HOLIDAYS

1 January: *Año Nuevo* (New Year's Day)
6 January: *Epifanía* (Epiphany)
28 February: *Día de Andalucía*
19 March: *San José*
Maundy Thursday: *Jueves Santo*
Good Friday: *Viernes Santo*
1 May: *Fiesta del Trabajo* (May Day/Labour Day)
Mid-June: Corpus Christi
15 August: *Asunción de Nuestra Señora* (Assumption Day)
12 October: *Día de la Hispanidad* (National Day)
1 November: *Todos los Santos* (All Saints' Day)
6 December: *Día de la Constitución* (Constitution Day)
8 December: *Día de la Inmaculada Concepción* (Immaculate Conception)
25 December: *Navidad*

LOCAL FESTIVALS & EVENTS

January
2 January: *Día de la Toma*, Granada. Celebration of the day the *Reyes Católicos* (Catholic Monarchs) entered the city.

First Sunday: *Romería de la Virgen del Mar* in Almería. The first of

25

many Andalusian pilgrimages held throughout the year.

5 January: Málaga hosts a spectacular horseback pageant (*Cabalgata de los Reyes Magos*).

February
First Sunday: a procession to the Sacromonte in Granada, accompanied by gypsy guitar music, takes place in honour of the city's patron saint, *San Cecilio*. At least half the city's population takes part.

During Lent various organizations in Málaga get together to arrange the *Carnaval* processions.

March/April
During *Semana Santa* (Holy Week) there are magnificent religious festivals all over Andalusia, indeed the whole of Spain. Málaga's ★ *Procession* involves 35 guilds hauling over 70 monumental figures throughout the streets of the city. The Easter processions in Granada are especially atmospheric.

May
At the beginning of the month many places in Andalusia display *cruces de mayo*, May crosses decked with flowers.

June
The *Feria de San Bernabé* in Marbella is held at the beginning of June, and is centred around equestrian events.

June/July
End of June/beginning of July: Granada hosts the popular ★ *Festival de Música y Danza de Granada*, an international festival of music and dance, featuring well-known

Traditional costumes and well-groomed horses are part and parcel of every fiesta

MARCO POLO SELECTION: FESTIVALS

1 Festival de Música y Danza in Granada
Renowned musicians and dancers perform in the Alhambra palace and the Generalife (page 26)

2 Easter procession in Málaga
The highlight of Semana Santa in Málaga is the elaborate and colourful Easter parade (page 26)

artists from the fields of classical music, jazz and ballet.

July
Early July: The *Feria y Fiesta Mayor* in Estepona, with horseback processions in traditional Andalusian costume.

Mid-July: the *Virgen del Carmen* sea procession in Fuengirola.

25 July: the Spanish patron saint's day, *Santiago Apóstol*, is celebrated not only in the Galician town of Santiago which bears his name, but throughout the rest of Spain.

August
Mid-August: one whole week is dedicated to the *Feria de Málaga*, held in the old town, with daily bullfights, stalls in the parks, and a party atmosphere until late into the night.

Mid-August: *Fiesta de la Recolección*, Antequera. Bullfights, street theatre, various sporting events, and a big cattle market.

Mid-August: *Fiesta de la Virgen de la Antigua* in Almuñecar. A parade of boats by night in honour of the town's patron saint.

Mid-August: *Feria de San Roque* in Torrox, well known for its fireworks.

Mid-August: *Flamenco festival* in Benalmádena in honour of Nuestra Señora de la Cruz.

Last week of August: *Feria* in Almería, along with an international music festival.

September
First two weeks in September: *Fiesta de la Virgen de la Peña* in Mijas. A wonderful spectacle of people in brightly-coloured costumes participating in flamenco and dancing competitions. This feria also features the *Encierro Taurino*, an event in which young bulls are driven through the streets.

First Thursday of the month: *Día del Turista* is celebrated in Torremolinos, with gaudy shows and cultural performances.

End September: *Feria de San Miguel* in Vélez-Málaga. Markets and a flamenco competition.

October
First Sunday and the three following days: folkloric performances at the *Feria* in Fuengirola.

November
International Jazz Festival in Almería.

December
On one Sunday in December, the traditional thanksgiving-style festival of *La Matanza* is celebrated with abandon in Pampaneira in the Alpujarras, during which hog roasts are the order of the day.

The Moorish inheritance

Spectacular, untamed mountains, cave dwellings and the Alhambra – the eighth wonder of the world

Little villages nestling on the slopes of the bare-topped mountains shimmer in the hazy light. The road leading up to them is full of potholes, and gradually dwindles to little more than a dust track. It leads through hilly countryside past estates and olive groves, and becomes ever more bumpy with increasingly hazardous ruts. Now reduced to a mountain track with no crash barriers to interrupt the views of the spectacular rocky cliffs, the rugged beauty of scree and fallen rocks incessantly eroded by the effects of the weather, the route is

The Generalife - a cool green paradise where the heat, noise and dust of the city seem worlds away

Hotel and restaurant prices

Hotels
Category 1: over 15 000 ptas
Category 2: 10 000-15 000 ptas
Category 3: below 10 000 ptas

Prices for two people sharing a double room with breakfast. If breakfast is not included, your best bet is to go to a café

Restaurants
Category 1: over 7000 ptas
Category 2: 4000-7000 ptas
Category 3: below 4000 ptas

Prices per person for an average quality three course meal, including a half-litre of house wine

Abbreviations

Avda.	*Avenida* (avenue)	**Pl.**	*Plaza* (square)
Ctra.	*Carretera* (trunk road)	**s/n**	*sin número* (no number)
C/.	*Calle* (road, street)	**Urb.**	*Urbanización* (residential area)

MARCO POLO SELECTION: GRANADA AND THE SIERRA NEVADA

1 Albaicín
Picturesque former Moorish district, very romantic in the twilight, with lovely views over the Alhambra and Sierra Nevada (page 31)

2 San Jerónimo
The tranquil inner courtyard of a monastery where you feel as if you could reach out and touch the past (page 38)

3 Patio de la Acequia in the Generalife
A courtyard with fountains and a variety of plants – the perfect place for peaceful contemplation (page 34)

4 Las Alpujarras
A wild mountain landscape on the southern slopes of the Sierra Nevada dotted with hidden villages (page 48)

more suited to mules than to cars. The landscape of the Sierra Nevada is wild and precipitous; melt water has eroded the soil and slate, and ground out deep gorges for itself. It is a wonder that people can live here at all. The barren soil where they grow their meagre crops is divided into small parcels of land, which rarely cover more than two or three hectares, spread across narrow terraces cut into the steeply sloping ground. These terraces, which enable the farmers to eke out their living, are an Arab invention. More than 600 years ago the Moors demonstrated how the clever use of irrigation could render an inhospitable region fertile. They may have been driven out, but they left their mark on the region, and many of their customs are still alive today in local traditions.

GRANADA

(F 1/H 3) The extent of the Arab influence is most in evidence in Granada (pop. 285000), which lies at the foot of the Sierra Nevada. Known as Elibyrge in the 5th century BC, and Iliberis in Roman times, it was transformed into a prosperous city by the Moors, who eventually made of it an independent kingdom which was to be the last bastion of Islam in Spain. The magnificent Alhambra, a complex of defensive structures, palaces and gardens developed during the Nasrid dynasty, is testimony to their artistic and architectural advancement and could justifiably claim the status of eighth wonder of the world. The city's old town, whose narrow streets and passages surround the Alhambra, is an architectural jewel, and Granada is considered by many to be Spain's most beautiful city.

Despite the fact that Granada has become such a major attraction, tourism seems to have been incorporated into daily life without stamping out traditional customs and values. A typical Sunday morning on the Plaza Nueva reflects this balance. Elderly ladies, some accompanied by their daughters, make their way to the cathedral. Elderly men, some accompanied by their sons, stand around the sloping square talking politics. Tourists flock to the newspaper kiosk to buy foreign newspapers. Buskers play classical guitar outside the Sibari restaurant. Joggers cross the square as part of their Sunday circuit. Eagle-eyed waiters stand guard, ready to pounce on passers-by and entice them to sit down for a coffee. The Plaza Nueva is one of Spain's most beautiful squares. Created as a central meeting place, it is the perfect place to watch the world go by, and absorb the atmosphere of the ancient city.

SIGHTS

Albaicín

★ ⬩ The Albaicín lies perched on a ridge of the Sierra de la Yedra to the north-west of the Alhambra. With its narrow streets and alleys and little hidden squares, Granada's oldest quarter resembles a typical Arab medina. Even the designs of the buildings have an Oriental feel to them. The villas, known as *carmenes,* are adorned with pots of colourful flowers, tiles laid in geometric patterns, ornamental plasterwork and jagged arches. Those in the *Calle de Pagues (Casa de los Mascarones)* and in the *Calle de Pardo (Casa Morisca)* are particularly charming, interspersed with tiny

Granada

200m

orchards and flights of steps hung with washing. The historic district is a labyrinth without signposts or a main street – you must put your faith in luck and a good sense of direction, but its higgledy-piggledy houses (which number almost three thousand) and apparently random layout are what gives it its charm. Today, the population of the Albaicín is around 12 000; in the 1960s three times as many people lived here. In 1994 it was designated a World Heritage Site by UNESCO. The central square, the *Plaza Larga*, is always bustling, while in the wide alleys off the *Calle del Agua*, the Albaicín is a world away from the noise and traffic of the city below, as peaceful as a rural hamlet. The sunset here, over the Alhambra with the Sierra Nevada in the background, has been described as 'A view unimaginable to anyone from the north' (Théophile Gaultier). The best place to see this spectacular sight is from the ✺ *Mirador de San Nicolás*, the terrace in front of the church of the same name. Although the Albaicín is not really a dangerous area, it always pays to be cautious.

Alhambra

The façades of this magnificent palace are like stone tapestries. Its walls are dazzlingly adorned with flowers, leaves and stars, intertwined with the name of Allah, carved thousands of times over in white marble. The whole of the Alhambra is covered in a rich embroidery of carved stone and lush greenery. Paths, flower beds and fountains are surrounded by green borders of laurel, jasmine and orange trees. Cypresses are clipped into the shapes of Arab gateways. Even the rose bushes are sculpted.

The best-preserved palace of the Islamic world is Spain's most popular attraction, drawing over two million visitors a year. Its clay brick walls, topped with green bushes, have as their backdrop the snow-capped mountains of the Sierra Nevada. The Arab name for it, *al hamra*, literally 'the red', derives from the reddish glow the walls take on in the evening light. After the *Reconquista* the Christian rulers built a mighty Renaissance palace within its grounds, but the pompous building is ill-matched to the filigreed masterpiece of Islamic architecture.

The oldest part of the Alhambra is the Alcazaba, which was built in the 9th century, long before the Nasrid era. Its watchtower, the ✺ *Torre de la Vela* (no. 57 on the plan) is 26 m high and affords a magnificent view across to the Sierra Nevada. In contrast, the ✺ *court between the Alcazaba and the Nasrid palace* is the best point from which to view the city, especially the Albaicín and Sacromonte districts. The *Mexuar*, the former audience and court chamber (13), was extended to form a chapel in Christian times. The most striking feature of the adjacent *Patio de los Arrayanes* (14), the Court of the Myrtles, is a long goldfish pond flanked by low myrtle hedges, with delicate arcades at each end. Dignitaries and envoys would have been conducted through here to the *Salón de Embajadores* (15), the Hall of the Ambassadors. This hall, on the ground floor of the *Torre de Comares* (16), was the palace's centre of power.

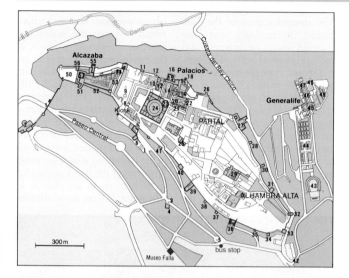

The Alhambra and the Generalife

1 Puerta de las Granadas
(Pomegranate Gate)
2 Torres Bermejas (Red Towers)
3 Fuente del Tomate (Tomato Fountain)
4 Monumento a Ganivet
(Monument to the Granadine writer)
5 Fuente del Pimiento
(Pepper fountain)
6 Pilar de Carlos V
(Charles V's column)
7 Puerta de la Justicia
(Gate of Justice)
8 Puerto del Vino (Wine Gate)
9 Plaza de los Aljibes
(Square of the cisterns)
10 Patio de Machuca
11 Torre de las Gallinas
(Tower of the Hens)
12 Torre de los Puñales
(Tower of the Daggers)
13 Mexuar (former audience chamber)
14 Patio de los Arrayanes
(Court of the Myrtles)
15 Salón de Embajadores
(Hall of the Ambassadors)
16 Torre de Comares
17 Habitaciones de Carlos V
(Apartments of Charles V)
18 Tocador de la Reina
(Queen's dressing room)

19 Sala de las Dos Hermanas
(Hall of the Two Sisters)
20 Patio de los Leones
(Court of the Lions)
21 Sala de los Abencerrajes
22 Sala de los Reyes
(Hall of the kings)
23 Crypt
24 Palacio de Carlos V
(Palace of Charles V)
25 Baños (Baths)
26 Torre de las Damas
27 Torre de los Picos
(Tower of the Battlements)
28 Torre del Cadí
29 Parador de San Francisco
30 Torre de la Cautiva (Tower of the Imprisoned Lady)
31 Torre de las Infantas
(Tower of the Infantas)
32 Torre del Cabo de la Carrera (Tower at the end of the racetrack)
33 Torre del Agua
(Water Tower)
34 Torre de Juan de Arce
35 Torre de Baltasar de la Cruz
36 Torre de Siete Suelos
(Tower of the Seven Storeys)
37 Torre del Capitán
(Captain's Tower)
38 Torre de las Brujas
(Witches' Tower)

39 Torre de las Cabezas
(Tower of the Heads)
40 Torre de Abencerrajes
41 Puerta de los Carros
(Gate of the Carts)
42 Entrance to the Generalife
43 Theatre
44 Jardines nuevos
(New gardens)
45 Pabellón Sur (South Pavilion)
46 Patio de la Acequia
(Court of the watercourse)
47 Pabellón Norte
(North Pavilion)
48 Patio de la Sultana
(Court of the Sultana)
49 Jardines altos
(Upper gardens)
50 Baluarte (bastion)
51 Torre de la Pólvora
(Powder tower)
52 Jardines de los Adarves
(Gardens of the battlements)
53 Torre Quebrada
(Broken tower)
54 Torre del Homenaje
(Tower of homage)
55 Torre de las Armas
(Tower of the Arms)
56 Torre de los Hidalgos
(Tower of the Nobles)
57 Torre de la Vela
(Watchtower)

The domed ceiling of the hall, almost 20 m high, was constructed from cedarwood and mother-of-pearl inlay. The central recess, opposite the entrance, housed the sultan's throne.

The *Patio de los Leones*, the Court of the Lions (20), the artistic heart of the Alhambra, forms part of the private royal quarters, and was originally a fragrant garden, with four channels conducting water from the four points of the compass to the centre representing the four rivers of the Islamic paradise. The twelve lions which disgorge the water collected at the centre, symbolic of the eternal waters of paradise, are made of black marble. 124 slim marble columns support the filigreed arcades. The numerous halls which surround the Court of the Lions are suffused with a timeless elegance and decorated with magical stylized scripts. Each of the halls from which the water flows out to the lion fountain has its own story. In the *Sala de los Abencerrajes* (21) on the south side,

Perfect symmetry and filigree marble in the Alhambra's Court of the Lions

the Sultan had 36 nobles of the Abencerraje clan put to death following a feast beneath the magnificent stalactite ceiling. The *Sala de las Dos Hermanas* (19), on the opposite side of the court, was the domain of the Sultana, the ruler's consort. One of the uppermost friezes contains extracts from Arabic scriptures, while the honeycomb vaulted ceiling consists of stalactites. The private chambers around the hall were for the use of the harem, where the ladies re-enacted their romances and traded intrigues. Apart from the concubines and their children, no mortal – with the exception of servants – was allowed to enter this private complex. The royal bedchamber, the *Sala de los Reyes* (22) is at the end of the Court of the Lions. It is unique for its hunting scenes and images of courtly life painted on leather – Islamic law forbids figurative representation of sentient beings.

Crossing the garden of the Patio de Lindaraja you come to the *Baños Árabes* (25), the Arab baths. Not far from the *Torre de las Damas* (26), a royal retreat with a five-arched portal fronted by a pond lined with laurels, oleanders and palms, are the terraced gardens of the Jardines del Partal, a fine example of harmony and beauty. The gardens are the starting point for a tour of the towers which formed the defences of the eastern part of the Alhambra.

Construction of the massive, square Renaissance *Palace of Charles V* (24) was begun in 1526 from plans drawn up by Pedro Machuca, but even after 42 years of work the building was still unfinished. One part which was

completed was the circular inner courtyard surrounded by galleries supported by Doric columns. Today it houses the *Museo de Bellas Artes* (*Tues-Sat 10.00-14.00*) and the *Museo de Arte Hispano-Musulmán* (*Tues-Sat 10.00-14.00*). The former focuses on the work of local artists, and the latter features collections of capitals, pottery and ceramics. The palace was reopened in 1995 following extensive restoration and renovation.

In winter daily 09.00-18.00, in summer Mon-Fri 09.00-20.00, Sat 09.00-22.00, Sun 09.00-18.00; Entrance: 625 ptas; Bus route 2

Cathedral of Santa María de la Encarnación/Capilla Real

This huge, ornate 16th-century stone edifice was designed by Diego de Siloé. Features by the architect include the richly-ornamented *Puerta del Perdón* and the *Puerta de San Jerónimo*, both on the north side. One of the great ecclesiastical buildings of Andalusia, it is also considered to be one of the most magnificent churches in the whole of Spain. The sculptor, painter and leading architect of the Granadine school, Alonso Cano (1601-67), contributed to its construction, which took nearly 200 years. He was responsible for the *west façade*. With its three monumental semicircular arches soaring to nearly the full height of the cathedral, the structure is reminiscent of an ancient Roman triumphal arch. Halfway up, a pronounced cornice divides the façade horizontally, and continues along the left-hand side of the square tower. This tower was originally intended to rise to 78 m, but was never completed, and was capped off at 60 m with a flat roof. The lower part of the tower housed Cano's workshops. His renown was such that he sometimes paid his creditors with sketches which were as valuable as cash.

The *interior* is 116 m in length, 67 m wide, and is divided into five aisles and a transept. Access to the cathedral is through the *Gran Vía de Colón* entrance. On entering, the first thing you set eyes on is the striking domed *Capilla Mayor*, a 48 m high stepped structure with beautiful 16th-century stained-glass windows. Conquering Granada in the name of Christianity, and driving out the last of the Moors from Europe, was the life's work of the powerful Spanish monarchs, Isabella of Castile and Ferdinand of Aragón; hence their desire to be buried here. Their mortal remains have lain in the Royal Chapel since 1521, when they were brought over from the Alhambra. Alongside are the tombs of their daughter, Juana la Loca (Joan the Mad) and her husband Philip the Fair; their simple lead coffins can be seen in the crypt. The tombs are made from Carrara marble carved with the incredibly lifelike figures of the monarchs. The double monument to Ferdinand and Isabella is by the Italian sculptor Domenico Fancelli. Another striking feature is the beautiful, gilded wrought-iron screen which encloses the chancel; it was made in 1520 and depicts various biblical scenes. The high altar by Felipe Bigarny portrays images of saints and scenes from the conquest of Granada. Queen Isabella's crown and sceptre are displayed in the sacristy by the mausoleum, along with Ferdinand's sword. A number of major works from the Queen's own collections, including some outstanding paintings by Flemish masters, also hang here. The late-Gothic chapel, built between 1505 and 1521 by Enrique de Egas, is entered via the medieval exchange building *(lonja)*.

In the 18th century the *Iglesia del Sagrario* was added to the cathedral. It was built on the site of the former mosque. Legend has it that during the siege of Granada in 1490 an old soldier, by the name of Hernán Pérez del Pulgar, rushed ahead of the Christian forces to Granada and headed straight for the mosque, where he nailed an *Ave Maria* to the door. His heroic deed is commemorated by a plaque on the front of the building. The present-day church was built between 1705 and 1759 in the Baroque style, and in addition to its marble altar it features a Renaissance stone font.

Cathedral and Capilla Real Mon-Sat 10.30-13.00 and 15.30-18.00, Sun afternoon only, no access to visitors during services, except for worship; Entrance: 250 ptas

Generalife

According to legend, this palace with its beautiful gardens on the hill across from the Alhambra was built by a Sultan for his son. The royal astrologers predicted that the prince's future would be a glorious one, provided he had no amorous encounters. In the light of this prophesy, the Sultan had the Generalife built so that his son could be brought up in splendid isolation. In such a refuge filled with roses, orange trees, jasmine and myrtles, the

The Carrara marble tomb of Ferdinand and Isabella

young prince would remain undistracted by the female sex, and so escape the emotional turmoil of falling in love.

The spacious complex is a masterpiece of garden design. The ✧ main promenade offers a unique view over the whole of the Alhambra that lies below. The small Moorish palace, with the gardens stretching out behind it, is reached by an avenue lined with cypresses which runs alongside the walls, punctuated by towers, and past the old Franciscan monastery.

The ★ *Patio de la Acequia* (Court of the Watercourse) is a tranquil place with its fountains and rich variety of plants; further out towards the cliff are the *Patio de los Cipreses* (Court of the Cypresses) and the *Escalera del Agua*, the beautiful 'water staircase', so-called because of the cool water that cascades down channels cut into the stone balustrades. In 1954 an open-air theatre, in the form of an amphitheatre, was built in the gardens which every summer provides the setting for a music and dance festival.
Same opening times as the Alhambra; Entrance: 625 ptas

Monasterio de la Cartuja

The church, sacristy, cloister and refectory of this 16th-century Carthusian monastery on the northern outskirts of the town are well preserved. The finely-detailed statue of St Bruno on the high altar in the main body of the church and the rich stucco ornamentation of the sacristy are examples of the ornate Spanish Baroque style known as *churri-gueresco*, at its most excessive. On the whole, although the monastery is gaudy and extravagant, its atmosphere is unique and its lavish decor demonstrates the extent of wealth enjoyed by the reclusive monks.
Mon–Sat 10.00-13.00 and 16.00-19.00, Sun afternoon only; Entrance: 200 ptas; Paseo de la Cartuja; Bus route 8

Sacromonte

This ancient gypsy district enjoys an elevated position, uphill from the Albaicín overlooking the Río Darro valley. The hill is dotted with cave dwellings, many of which are still inhabited by gypsies. The precise origin of Granada's *gitanos* is unknown, but it is thought they obtained their right of domicile here as a reward for supporting the Christian victors after the recapture of Granada. Today they are an integral part of the city and its identity. The flamenco performances staged by them in the caves of the district are aimed at tourists, but their renditions of the melancholy *canto jondo*, the form of song upon which flamenco is based, are heart-breakingly intense.

On the first Sunday in February, the traditional Sacromonte pilgrimage up to the 17th-century *Abadía del Sacromonte (Mon-Sat 10.00-12.00, Sun 10.00-19.00)* takes place. From the top of the hill the ☙ panoramic view of the Alhambra, floodlit at night, with the mountains behind and the city at its feet, is lovely. To reach the 'holy mountain' cross the Plaza Nueva, follow the Carrera del Darro and the Cuesta del Chapiz, then turn right along the cactus-lined Camino del Sacromonte.

San Jerónimo

★ This monastery complex with its unusual fountain lies a few hundred metres north-west of the Plaza Bib-Rambla. It was the first Christian church to be consecrated after the Moors were driven out (1496). Completed in 1547 by Diego de Siloé, it is considered to be one of the most magnificent Renaissance ecclesiastical buildings in Spain.
Mon-Sat 10.00-13.30 and 16.00-19.00, Sun afternoons only; Entrance: 200 ptas; Calle Rector López Argüeta 9

University

Granada's university is one of Spain's most distinguished, and is attended by 45 000 students. The main building, formerly a Jesuit college dating back to the 18th century and now housing the Faculty of Law, is to the west of the cathedral in the Calle San Jerónimo. To the east of it, just behind the cathedral stands the Madraza, the former Moorish university. In 1500 it was converted into a town hall, and it was later remodelled with a Baroque façade, which it retains to this day, but which conceals a fine Moorish interior.

MUSEUMS

Casa de los Tiros

This museum is dedicated to the history of Granada, and documents the city's past with engravings and plans, sculptures and photographs. The collection is augmented with furniture, ceramics, brass artefacts, textiles and other traditional crafts. The architecture of this 16th-century building, reminiscent of a castle with an inner patio, is delightful.
Mon-Sat 10.00-14.00 Entrance: 200 ptas; Calle Pavaneras/Plaza del Padre Suárez

Lorca's summer house

The writer and poet Federico García Lorca, whose works have so much significance to Andalusians, lived out in the country, but he had a summer house in Granada which has recently been renovated and is now open to the public.

Tues-Sun 10.00-13.00 and 17.00-20.00; Entrance: 200 ptas; Huerta de San Vicente 6

Museo de la Abadía del Sacromonte

This museum on the Sacromonte features a number of works by important Spanish artists, a collection of manuscripts, which mostly date from the Arab occupation, and some interesting miniature books.

Tues-Sat 10.00-12.00, Sun 10.00-19.00, Entrance: 200 ptas

Museo Arqueológico

The many finds from archaeological sites both in and around Granada are gathered together here – from prehistoric, Roman, Visigothic, but predominantly Moorish, times.

Tues-Sat 10.00-14.00, Entrance: 200 ptas; Carrera del Darro 43

Parque de las Ciencias

This interactive museum, developed by the University and sponsored by various banks, provides an insight into the latest scientific discoveries. It is divided into numerous sections including the environment, ecology, sustainable economy, and the ozone layer. Use an erosion monitor to observe the effects of rainfall on planted and bare soil, or observe the skies through a telescope. There is a separate section for children under 7.

Mon-Sat 10.00-19.00, Sun 10.00-15.00, Entrance: 200 ptas; Avenida Mediterráneo s/n

RESTAURANTS, CAFÉS & TAPAS BARS

The narrow streets and squares of Granada are full of good, relatively cheap restaurants and tapas bars. There are, of course, the inevitable tourist traps to watch out for.

Alhambra

A good place to try that Spanish classic, *chocolate con churros* – deep-fried doughnut sticks with a cup of thick hot chocolate.

Daily (closed mid-afternoon 14.00-17.00); Calle Mesones 25

Bogavante

Meat dishes and desserts made according to old Arabic recipes.

Closed Sun; Calle Duende 15; Tel: (958) 25 91 12; Category 1-2

La Castellana

This *bocadillería*, with its brightly painted interior, walls covered with mirrors and inscriptions, long counter and gallery, fine furniture and huge hams hanging from the ceiling, comes as a pleasant surprise in a street full of dull buildings.

Camino de Ronda 100

Chikito

This was once the regular haunt of *El Rinconcillo*, the literary circle of which Lorca was a member. Wonderful choice of tapas.

Closed Weds; Plaza del Campillo 9; Tel: (958) 22 33 64; Category 2

Colombia

Near the Alhambra, this *restaurante típico* is an appealing combination of Mozarabic design and Andalusian cuisine. You certainly pay for the magnificent surroundings, but it isn't every day

you get to eat somewhere like this. Worth treating yourself to.
Daily (except Sun); Calle Antequeruela Baja 1; Tel: (958) 22 74 33; Category 2

Cunini
Fresh fish guaranteed, prepared in a variety of ways.
Daily (except Mon); Pescadería 14; Tel: (958) 25 07 77; Category 2

Helados Jijonenca
The place for ice cream. Among the local specialities are the *turrón*, an excellent nougat ice cream, and the *horchata de chufa*, made of almond milk.
Carrera del Genil 97

El Ladrillo
❖ A great bar on a little square in the Albaicín. The only item on the menu is *pescados fritos*: fried fish served with a crisp salad. A favourite haunt among the locals.
Placeta Fátima; Category 3

Lisboa
✻ Young clientele who come here to chat and flirt. The cake counter and the lovely view of the Plaza Nueva are equally enticing.
Calle Reyes Católicos 65

Café-Pastelería López-Mezquita
The front of the premises is an old-fashioned shop whose shelves are full of glass jars filled with all kinds of sweets. At the back is a stylish marble-clad coffee house which offers a mouthwatering selection of pastries, both savoury and sweet.
Calle Reyes Católicos 41

La Manigua
Good food in a respectable establishment. The unobtrusive service matches the subdued lighting.
Daily (except Sun); Puerta Real 1; Tel: (958) 22 77 22; Category 2

Los Manueles
The atmosphere is sombre: heavy beams, dark curtains and hundreds of hams hanging from the ceiling. The *tortilla al sacromonte*, however, is remarkably light.
Calle Zaragoza 2-4; Tel: (958) 22 34 13; Category 2

Mirador de Morayma
↘↗ Good-value food with a splendid view of the Alhambra thrown in. The desserts made by the nuns of the Zafra convent are quite literally, heavenly.
Daily (except Sun); Calle Pianista García Carrillo 2; Tel: (958) 22 82 90; Category 2

Pilar del Toro
Tasty regional cooking, with wholesome local dishes such as *habas a la granadina*, broad beans with ham. A wide choice of delicacies is offered at the counter.
Hospital Santa Ana 12; Tel: (958) 22 38 47; Category 2

Sibari
Popular with tourists, especially with the Japanese, who can study the substantial menu in their own language. This traditional restaurant in the heart of town has plenty of available seating outside on the square.
Plaza Nueva 3; Tel: (958) 22 77 56; Category 2

Victoria
An extensive menu, sizeable portions, reasonable prices and fast service.
Puerta Real 3; Tel: (958) 25 77 04; Category 2

The Alhambra parador - must be booked well in advance

SHOPPING

Antiques
La Diligencia: a small shop crammed with antique furniture.
Calle Reyes Católicos 63

Centro Comercial Arabial
Vast shopping centre.
Mon-Sat 10.00-21.00; Calle Arabial 93-97

Ceramics
For Arabesque tiles in beautiful designs and colours, try the ceramics shop on the *Plaza Isidoro*.

Crafts
Handicrafts, some made by the rural population of the Alpujarras, are sold in the *Corral del Car-* *bón* by the *Asociación de Artesanos del Albaicín*. During the Moorish era, this former *caravanserai* served as a kind of inn and market place combined. The livery stable was in the inner courtyard, and now houses the showrooms; the floor where the traders lodged now accommodates *artespaña*, a craft workers cooperative.

Fashion
Cortefiel is a large fashion boutique in a baroque house. The façade is floodlit at night.
Plaza de Isabel la Católica/Gran Vía de Colón

Flamenco instruments
Along with the usual classical instruments you will also find

41

handmade concert guitars for flamenco from 70 000 ptas.
Cuesta de Gomérez

Maps

Walkers and mountaineers can
get detailed maps of the Sierra
Nevada from the *Instituto Geográ-
fico Nacional, Avenida Divina Pastora* 7.

Souvenirs

Lying in the shadow of the cathedral the *Alcaicería* is a temple to
kitsch. The market is made up
of rows of small shops and
stalls, tightly packed together,
selling everything from flamenco
costumes and painted pottery
cottages to lockets, castanets and
countless other bright and
colourful, but completely super-
fluous items. In Moorish times
this spot was occupied by the silk
market and the place still retains
something of the atmosphere
of an Oriental souk.

ACCOMMODATION

Albergue Juvenil Granada

Youth hostel with TV room,
library and garden. The main
drawback is that lights go out at
23.30 sharp.
*74 beds; Camino de Ronda 171; Tel:
(958) 27 26 38*

Albergue Juvenil Viznar

Youth hostel with a swimming
pool. Up in the mountains, just
7 km outside Granada.
*100 beds; Camino de Fuente Grande
s/n, 18179 Viznar; Tel: (958) 49
03 07*

Alixares del Generalife

Hotel with swimming pool and
piano bar next to one of the
world's most famous gardens.
*170 rooms; Avenida de los Alixares;
Tel: (958) 22 55 75, Fax: 22 41 02;
Category 2-3*

América

Cosy hotel with just 13 rooms
and an intimate atmosphere.
Breakfast is served on a typical
Andalusian patio.
*Real de la Alhambra 53; Tel: (958)
22 74 71, Fax: 22 74 70; Category 2*

Camping Los Álamos

Clean, with shady trees and
swimming pool, though you can
hear the hum of traffic from the
main road.
*200 pitches; April-Oct; N342, 6 km
out of the city; Tel: (958) 20 84 79*

Camping Reina Isabel

♨ Probably the best-run campsite in or around Granada. Clean,
with swimming pool and good-
value restaurant, and the added
attraction of beautiful views of
the Alhambra and the Sierra
Nevada.
*230 pitches; Mar-Oct; Carretera de
Zubia, 4 km out of the city; Tel: (958)
59 00 41*

Casablanca

A simple *hotel residencia* with lots
of brass and plush, but unbeatable
value for money.
*49 rooms; Calle Frailes 5; Tel: (958)
25 76 00; Category 3*

Gran Vía Granada

A post-modern building on the
city's main arterial route, with
marble decor and a practical underground garage. The large ✪ ☂
restaurant is a favourite with the
locals, and draws a young crowd,
largely because of the cheap
menu.

85 rooms; Gran Vía de Colón 25; Tel: (958) 28 54 64, Fax: 28 55 91; Category 2-3

Macía

Simple guest house in a superb location with typical Andalusian interior.

44 rooms; Plaza Nueva 4; Tel: (958) 22 75 36, Fax: 28 55 91; Category 2

Las Nieves

A cheap hostel in the lower part of town. The food is cooked by the landlady herself.

22 rooms; Calle Sierpe Baja 5; Tel: (958) 26 53 11, Fax: 26 53 51; Category 3

Parador de Granada

Built for Isabella of Castile, this former convent was renovated in 1995. Guests have the Alhambra to themselves at night and early in the morning.

35 rooms; Real de la Alhambra; Tel: (958) 22 14 40, Fax: 22 22 64; Category 1

Rooms agency

Information on cheap rooms can be obtained from the rooms and arranged lifts agency, *Mon-Fri 11.00-13.00 and 17.00-20.00; Calle Elvira 85; Tel: (958) 29 29 20.*

Victoria

A listed building in a lovely location. Efficient service, beautiful lounges, and rooms with wonderfully old-fashioned furnishings.

62 rooms; Puerta Real 3; Tel: (958) 25 77 00, Fax: 26 31 08; Category 3

SPANISH LANGUAGE COURSES

♯ There are a number of Spanish language courses on offer in summer in Granada, mainly aimed at young people (minimum length 1 week). For further information contact the *Información Juvenil, Calle Varela 4; Tel: (958) 22 20 52.*

Another good way to get to know the locals is to study alongside them. The *Escuela Montalbán,* only ten minutes' walk from the centre, offers a variety of language courses. Foreigners come here to learn Spanish, and Spaniards come here to learn other languages in neighbouring classrooms; it's a truly multilingual campus. The courses are practical, and cover a range of abilities from beginners to advanced. The mornings are for studying, while the afternoons are set aside for excursions and putting the lessons into practice.

For further information on Spanish courses contact: *Don Quijote UK, 2-4 Stoneleigh Park Rd, Stoneleigh, Epsom, Surrey, KT190 QR; Tel: 0181 786 8081* or *Euro Academy Outbound, 77A George Street, Croydon, CRO 1LD; Tel: 0181 686 2363.*

SPORT & LEISURE

Flamenco course

The *Carmen de las Cuevas* flamenco school offers a standard 5-day course for 5000 ptas and a 5-day intensive course for 19 500 ptas. Board and lodging can also be provided on request.

Carmen de las Cuevas, Cuesta de los Chinos 15, 18010 Granada; Tel: (958) 22 10 62, Fax: 22 04 76

Golf

The *Granada Club de Golf* has an excellent 18-hole course 27 km outside the city at Las Gabias. *Tel: (958) 58 07 2; 4000 ptas*

Mountaineering

The *Federación Andaluza de Montañismo* arranges contacts for mountain-climbers, and organizes excursions.
Camino de Ronda 101, Edificio Atalaya 1, Oficina 76, 18003 Granada; Tel: (958) 29 13 40

Riding

Treks take you into the heart of the Sierra Nevada, through the Alpujarras, along the Costa Granadina, and as far as Almería. Accommodation is provided in wayside inns and on *cortijos* (country estates). Guides are available if required.
Cabalgar Rutas Alternativas, Rafael Belmonte, 18412 Bubión; Tel: (958) 76 61 46 and 76 60 22

Swimming

If the sea feels too far away, you can always go for a swim in the *Piscina Cubierta Arabial*, an indoor public pool in the centre of town.
Mon-Sat 11.30-22.00, Sun 11.30-14.00; Entrance: 450 ptas; Calle Arabial s/n

Tennis

Pistas de Tenis Neptuno; Calle Arabial s/n; Tel: (958) 25 10 55; 700 ptas per hour

Walking

Viajes Granatur runs walking tours to the mountains and regions south of Granada with qualified guides. Study packs are provided.
Calle Fontiveros 42; Tel: (958) 12 43 91

Winter sports

Information on winter sports is available from the *Federación Andaluza de Deportes de Invierno.*
Calle Arabial 32, 18003 Granada; Tel: (958) 25 07 05 and 25 08 62

ENTERTAINMENT

Bar Enrique

❀ A typical Andalusian bar, good atmosphere, and delicious tapas.
Acera del Darro 8

Calderería Nueva

⚹ This stepped passage, free from cars, is popular for its numerous bars and cheap tearooms. There is always something going on here, whatever the time of day or year. When the weather is warm, tables and chairs are strewn over the uneven cobblestones, cats rub up against the legs of people seated there, and there is usually someone strumming a guitar somewhere. The most interesting places are: *A Zahara (no. 12)*, where the air is full of incense and you can sip mint tea in the souk-like surroundings; *Tetería Alfaguara (no. 7)*, good for fruit juices and milk drinks; *Tetería as Surat (no. 5)*, with wall hangings, lanterns, small tables inlaid with quotations from the Koran and Arabic music; *Tetería Café (no. 24)*, where you sit on low stools around flat tables savouring a wide choice of teas and delicious Oriental sweets.

Calle Pedro Antonio de Alarcón

⚹ This bar and the surrounding streets are the hub of student social life. Beer (*caña*) is served on tap, red wine by the glass, and the tapas are the best value for money.

Castaneda

❀ A large bar, full to bursting every evening with a crowd which is largely made up of academics and business people enjoying generous cold platters of ham

and cheese with good wine. Loud, bustling and authentic, this bar is a local favourite.
Placeta de San Gil 6/Calle Elvira

Cinema

New releases are shown at the *Astoria (Avenida de la Constitución)*. The *Multicentro (Solarillo de Gracia 9)* is a 7-screen complex.

El Conventillo

A late-night bar for nocturnals.
Daily 20.00-04.00; Calle Cedrán 7

Flamenco and folklore

Not everything in Granada advertised as flamenco is the real thing. In the whitewashed gypsy caves of the Sacromonte, the Andalusian flamenco shows are often dismal affairs. It's a matter of luck as to whether you see a show which has something of the true power and passion of flamenco; *Jardines Neptuno in the Calle Arabial, s/n; Tel: (958) 25 11 12* is one of the best places to try – the company is led and choreographed by Mariquilla, a teacher of 'flamencology'.

'Granada by night with dinner and flamenco show' is a short tour of the city, followed by an evening meal at the *El Corral del Príncipe (Mon-Sat 20.00-daybreak; Plaza Mayor 1; Tel: (958) 22 80 88; Category 2-3)*, and ending with a show. After midnight, guests are taken back to their hotels or dropped off in the city centre.
Price: 3500-6500 ptas; Tel: (958) 22 80 88, Fax: 51 86 66;

El Fogón

❖ One of the most popular tapas bars, always full but not cheap.
Calle de Navas 27

Granada 10

♱ Mega-disco, always full.
Tues-Sun 22.30-04.00; Calle Cárcel Baja 13

Ruida Rosa

♱ This daily disco only runs until midnight.
Calle Sol 18

Granada's city centre bustles with activity day and night

Snooker

❖ Comfortable leather arm-chairs, solid snooker tables and a long bar characterize the *Club de Billar*. Music and the continuous babble of the TV are part of the atmosphere. Chess and other board games also available.
Daily 21.30-02.00; Calle de Gran Capitán 25

Teatro Estable de Granada

This tiny theatre stages productions in Spanish only, but there is an international theatre festival in May.
Calle de Gran Capitán 16; Tel: (958) 20 27 25; Programme information Tel: (958) 22 00 22

La Tertulia

❖ This bar is a favourite haunt for Granada's tango dancers.
Calle Pintor López Mezquita

INFORMATION

Oficina de Turismo

Plaza de Mariana Pineda 10, 18012 Granada; Tel: (958) 22 66 88, Fax: 22 89 16; Corral del Carbón, 18001 Granada; Tel: (958) 22 59 90, Fax: 22 89 18; both open Mon-Fri 10.00-13.30 and 16.30-19.00, Sat 10.00-13.00

SURROUNDING AREA

Casa Museo de Federico García Lorca in Fuente Vaqueros (F 1/G 3)

Schoolchildren, students, and visitors from the world over make the pilgrimage to Lorca's birthplace 20 km north-west of Granada to pay homage to one of the most important writers and poets of the 20th century. His use of language and feel for rhythm have influenced a generation of poets and inspired millions of readers. Here, in his parents' house, the collection of documents tell of his tragically short life (1898-1936). Lorca was a man of the people, and was especially fascinated by gypsies. Despite his claims that he was apolitical, he was kidnapped by a group of Franco's supporters during the civil war and taken to the little village of Viznar near Granada, where he was shot and buried in an unknown location; to this day his grave has not been found. The pictures, furniture, manuscripts with their ink-blots and scrawled writing, and general atmosphere of the house evoke the life of a great poet.
April-Sept 10.00-13.00 and 18.00-20.00, Oct-Mar 10.00-13.00 and 16.00-18.00, Entrance: 200 ptas; Calle Poeta García Lorca 4; an hourly bus service runs from the train station in Avenida de Andaluces

Galera (L 1)

This village (pop. 1600) in the north of the province of Granada, situated among mountains and natural parks, is 150 km away from the city. It may be off the beaten track, but the journey is worthwhile. Here in the green valley between two rivers you can even rent one of the cave dwellings cut out of the white rock. The caves are equipped with electricity and running water, and are particularly suited to walkers: the tourist office in Galera has details of at least ten routes which lead to places of interest in the surrounding countryside. You can be accompanied by a guide, and hire a donkey or a bicycle. If you are looking for a bit of peace and quiet after the hustle

The cave dwellings of Guadix are like a surreal film set

and bustle of Granada, you will certainly find it here. The peace and stillness of the area is astounding. The inhabitants of Galera are friendly and welcoming, the wine cellars are well-stocked with good local wines and the menus full of hearty meat and vegetable stews. The price of renting a cave dwelling ranges between 6000 ptas (for a cave that sleeps four) and 9500 ptas (for eight); the minimum stay is two nights.

Information and bookings: Promociones Turísticas de Galera, Avenida Nicasio Tomás 12, 18840 Galera; Tel: and Fax: (958) 73 90 68

Guadix   (I 2)

The steep tufa rocks of this region have long been inhabited. Around one quarter of this town's 20000 population still live in underground caves. The modern-day cave dwellings are surprisingly spacious and comfortable. They are characterized by their whitewashed façades, chimneys and television aerials that rise out of the ground above. The most interesting troglodyte settlement is 6 km to the north-west of the town at *Purullena.* The main street here is lined with shops selling local pottery and ceramics. It is not easy to see inside one of the houses in the *barrio troglodita;* if you do receive an unsolicited invitation, always make sure that money is not going to be demanded after your visit. Guadix was founded by the Romans under Julius Caesar, and the Moors built a castle here which is now open to visitors *(daily 09.00-13.00 and 16.00-18.00; Entrance: 200 ptas).* Go to the ☜ top of the hill for the best view of this unusual landscape of bizarre rock formations and caves, along with remains of the town walls.

Loja   (E 1)

The white houses of Loja (pop. 20000) are clustered on a hillside that leads down to the Río Genil. This typically Andalusian town is renowned for its romantic little streets and the well-preserved remains of a 10th-century Moorish *Alcazaba* that stands proudly on the hill above. Buildings of interest include the churches of *San Gabriel* (1552) with its cupola, and *Santa María* (16th century) with its

Baroque façade. 20 km west of the town is the luxury hotel complex of *La Bobadilla (60 rooms; Apartado 52, 18300 Loja; Tel: (958) 32 18 61, Fax: 32 18 10; Category 1)*. Modelled on a typical Andalusian village it was built in the historic *mudéjar* style (a Moorish style of architecture). The reception hall is based on the design of a mosque, and many of the rooms are furnished with Andalusian rustic furniture and feature ceramic tiled floors and marble-clad baths. All the ✲ bedrooms have terraces and an extensive view over the green hills. There is also a restaurant.

SIERRA NEVADA

(H-I 3-4) This mountain range to the south-east of Granada is the highest on the Iberian peninsula. The cold, dry Sierra wind blows across the wild landscape with its huge rock formations, making it hard to believe that the Mediterranean coast is only 60 km away.

From 2000 m up the small-leaved cushion plants begin to disappear, and only a few thorn bushes manage to cling to the slopes. This is the roof of Andalusia. On a clear day you can make out the contours of the African coast and the Straits of Gibraltar from here. This is Europe's most southerly skiing region, where snow is usually guaranteed from December until April. A journey through this wonderful landscape which has snow all year round in parts, yet which boasts a Mediterranean climate, is a rich and varied experience.

PLACES OF INTEREST IN THE SIERRA NEVADA

Las Alpujarras　　　　　**(H-I 4)**
★ The mountains with their sparse vegetation roll like huge waves towards the Mediterranean. Spain's highest settlements lie here in the southern part of the Sierra Nevada. They cling to the steep mountainsides

Bubión has a number of typical Andalusian bungalows to let

and all face southwards. Their houses are square with flat roofs made from a waterproof, slate-like clay. They are arranged in steps, and are so close together that they share their component parts — the roof of one house is the terrace of its neighbour above. For a good overview of the architectural legacy of the Moors take a trip along the C 333 road. You will pass a number of interesting places: *Lanjarón* with its trout stream and lovely thermal baths (*May-Nov; Tel: (958) 77 01 37*); *Orgiva, Cañar,* a tiny village with well-preserved Moorish houses surrounded by oak, chestnut and pine forests; *Pampaneira* and *Bubión,* both situated in a fertile valley with orchards, meadows, walnut and chestnut trees; *Capileira, Trevélez,* which lies at a height of 1580 m, in a deep, tree-lined valley, its mountain streams teeming with trout; and *Pórtugos, Bérchules* and *Ugíjar.*

In contrast to the northern side of the Sierra Nevada, the Alpujarras to the south seem even more unspoilt: here is a truly wild high mountain landscape which barely tolerates human habitation. After the Christian reconquest, quite a few reserved, taciturn, Galician farmers settled here. In these hidden villages, the income per capita is the lowest in Andalusia and there is an alarmingly high rate of illiteracy. In the autumn, tourists can come to help with the *murraca,* the chestnut harvest, or the apple-picking, and to learn how the fields are traditionally cultivated with the help of mules and powerful oxen.

Between Capileira and Pampaneira are the *Villas Turísticas de Bubión (136 rooms; Tel: (958) 76 31 12, Fax: 76 31 36; Category 2),* holiday bungalows built in the Alpujarreño style. In Pórtugos, good accommodation is available in the country hotel of *Nuevo Malagueño (30 rooms; Carretera Orgiva-Trevélez; Tel: (958) 76 60 98;Category 3). Dallas Love Sierra Trails in Pampaneira (Calle Verónica s/n; Tel: (958) 76 30 38)* arrange four-wheel-drive and riding tours. The *Club Global* in *Bubión* has long experience in organising hiking and riding tours; they also hire out mountain bikes and provide experienced guides. Climbers of all abilities, including beginners, can also obtain advice and infomation here *(Carretera de Capileira s/n; Tel: (958) 76 30 54, Fax: 76 32 36).* Good, hearty peasant fare is served in *Bubión* in the *Algaja (Calle Estación 4; Tel: (958) 76 31 31; Category 3),* in *Capileira* at the *Finca Los Llanos (Carretera Sierra s/n; Tel: (958) 76 30 71; Category 3),* in *Orgiva* in the *Alpujarras-Grill (Carretera Trevélez s/n; Tel: (958) 78 55 49; Category 2),* in *Pampaneira* at the *Restaurante Alfonso (Calle José Antonio 1; Tel: (958) 76 30 02; Category 3)* and in *Trevélez* at the *Restaurante Alvarez (Plaza Francisco Abellán; Tel: (958) 76 50 03; Category 2-3).*

If you want to take a regional speciality home with you, buy some of the exquisite locally cured ham which is sold in all of the mountain villages. *Jamón serrano* is hung and dried for over a year in the high mountain air. One kilo costs between 1000 and 1500 ptas, depending on how long the ham has been hanging.

Pampaneira has become a refuge for young craftspeople, far away from the noise of the holiday resorts. It is a good place to pick up an original souvenir. You can even try your own hand at working the clay at the *Finca Castillo San Rafael* by the sea. Michael Still, an English émigré, runs art and ceramics courses here all year round (*Castillo San Rafael, La Herradura, Tel: (958) 64 02 47, Fax: 64 02 69).*

The Sierra Nevada can also be explored by mountain bike, climbing as much as 800 metres per day on rough dirt tracks and mule trails; the ultimate goal is *Cabo de Gata* near Almería.

Accommodation in the pueblos of the Alpujarras can be booked via the owners' association, *RAAR (Red Andaluza de Alojamientos Rurales)*, a non-commercial reservation service, at *Apartado de Correos 2035, 04080 Almería; Tel: (950) 26 50 18 (Spanish and French only), Fax: 27 04 31 (English also)*. Bookings must be for a minimum of two days, but you have the advantage of living with a family and learning about the everyday agricultural life of the area. Breakfast or half board are available by arrangement. The holiday accommodation is extremely varied, from a traditional house with no electricity in the middle of nowhere to a well-appointed country residence; most in price category 3.

There is a daily bus excursion to the Alpujarras from Granada *(Tel: (958) 22 59 90).*

Mulhacén/Pico de Valeta (H 3-4)

In summer the Sierra Nevada boasts the most pleasant climate in Andalusia, perfect for touring the mountains. If you take the N 323 from Granada to the coast and turn off at the 27 km mark you will come on to the winding C 333. 16 km past Lanjarón you will reach the GR 421. Take the left turn just beyond the village of Pampaneira which will lead you on to the highest mountain road in Europe (only passable in summer). The first stunning sight reached by this steeply-climbing track is the *Laguna de la Caldera,* a crystal-clear mountain lake at a height of 2800 m. This hollow in the rock filled with melt water is a popular starting point for climbing *Mulhacén,* the highest peak on the Iberian peninsula (3482 m). Even if you are not used to mountain climbing, the ascent should only take around 60 minutes, provided you are reasonably fit. Those dedicated to outdoor pursuits can camp by the blue-green shimmering lake. The snow never completely disappears here, even in summer, and at night the temperature falls below freezing. With a set of good tyres you can continue along the uneven road by car until you reach the summit of *Pico de Veleta* (3398 m). At the top there is a pyramid of roughly-hewn stone crowned by the *Virgen de las Nieves,* a statue of the Madonna and (warmly wrapped) child. The view from here is stunning.

Solynieve/ Pradollano ski resort (H 3)

Since the slopes of Veleta have become popular for winter sports, this area, 30 km south-east of Granada, has developed into a thriving holiday resort with hotels and apartment blocks providing a total of 12 000 beds. The central resort of Pradollano (2100 m) is not the most picturesque of places, but its design is practical. It has 34 pistes and 20 ski lifts, including one of the most modern cable cars in Europe, which can transport up to 27 000 skiers per hour. The 61 km of pistes are well maintained and safe, making it an ideal area for beginners. There are deep snow routes, cross-country courses, and two ski stadia, as well as facilities for snowboarding, monoskiing and hang-gliding. The service and information centre of Solynieve (literally 'Sun and Snow') lies at a height of 2230 m; ski coaches and mountain guides can be booked from here. March and April are the best months for skiing, when there is the most snow. Needless to say, wherever Spaniards gather together, a lively nightlife is guaranteed. Around 30 restaurants, taverns, bars and discos come to life every evening, but not before midnight. This means that in the mornings the pistes are pleasantly clear and free.

A day pass costs 3500 ptas (six-day passes cost 15 600 ptas) and can be obtained at any *Escuela Oficial* or from *Telemark*. Piste maps to help you plan your route are provided with the pass. Skis can be hired at a weekly rate of around 10 000 ptas, and there are a substantial number of ski schools to choose from.

For updates on snow and weather conditions in the Sierra Nevada, call the weather information service on *(958) 24 91 00 and 48 01 53*.

Many of the restaurants are closed in summer. Among those that stay open are: the ✪ *Alpino (Tel: (958) 48 11 12; Category 3)*, a popular pizza restaurant which welcomes families with children; *El Nogal*, where you can sample the delicious traditional peasant dish *migas*, ham coated in breadcrumbs and cooked in garlic

(Tel: (958) 48 48 36); or the *Pourquoi Pas*, a well run establishment that serves a variety of international cuisine *(Tel: (958) 48 03 07; Category 2)*.

There is a central reservation service for accommodation *(Central de Reservas Sierra Nevada Club, Agencia de Viajes; Tel: (958) 24 91 11, Fax: 48 06 06)*. Bear in mind that many hotels are also closed in summer.

If you want to get to this area from Granada but do not have a car, there is a fast and reliable bus service run by the *Bonal* company: *Departures at 09.00 from Granada, Avenida de la Constitución; (tickets from the El Ventorillo bar near the Palacio de Congresos); return from Pradollano at 17.00.*

The Sierra Nevada was first set up for winter sports after World War II, and most people come here for the skiing. But the area is also an interesting place for keen walkers and nature lovers. Hikers can explore the chalky mountain scenery with the help of maps and leaflets from the information offices. The slopes of the Parque Natural de Sierra Nevada are a unique rock garden where as many as 67 endemic plants, unique to the region, thrive. These mountains are also the habitat for martens, badgers, foxes and golden eagles. Spotting a golden eagle while skiing down a wide valley is an unforgettable experience. It's hard to believe that you are on the same latitude as Tunisia. From these mountain tops you can see the 100 km long chain of the Sierra Nevada stretching out on either side of you, and the Mediterranean sparkling down below, unbelievably only an hour's drive away.

Africa in Europe

*Whitewashed villages and a genuine desert,
a region waking up to its full potential*

The landscape east of Andalusia is chalky-white and dotted with villages that look like Berber settlements transplanted from the high Atlas mountains to Europe. Only the minarets are missing. These isolated villages are surrounded by sparse mountains, desert dunes, swathes of esparto grass, and plains bathed in light: a lunar landscape interspersed with earthy greens and browns. Tropical fruits are cultivated on terraced fields that are scattered across the land from altitudes of 2000 m all the way down to the sea. The coastal region between Almuñecar and Almería is one of the sunniest on the Mediterranean, with an average of 3000 hours of sunshine per year. Its agricultural productivity is unique in Europe; the area is blanketed with vast hothouses formed by miles of plastic sheeting, particularly on the flat lands west of the Sierra de Gádor. These fertile fields lie alongside

Salobreña, with its winding passages and flights of steps, is the Granadines' favourite resort

areas of desert which are like something out of a western. Many westerns have in fact been made on location here – even *Lawrence of Arabia* was filmed here. The Sierra de Alhamilla is the only true desert in Europe.

The locals are gradually awakening to the economic potential of tourism, though the region has long been used as a bridge to Africa, operating regular ferry crossings to Morocco. The geographical proximity to the far continent, combined with the character of the people, was what led the Spanish writer Juan Goytisolo to dub this province 'Africa in Europe'.

ALMERIA

(L 4) Once the hideout for notorious pirates, over the centuries Almería has developed into one of the most important ports in Spain. Great quantities of merchandise were already being shipped from here in the Middle Ages; nowadays the main exports are ore, fish and fruit. Almería (pop. 160 000) has had a colourful past, and was constantly under threat of invasion by pirates from the sea and armies advancing from the landward side. Throughout its history the city has been conquered, lost, reconquered, surrendered again, and subjected to the vagaries of more than one anarchistic regime.

The city's turbulent past is reflected in the defensive structure of many of its historic buildings – even the cathedral resembles a Christian fortress. In comparison with the towns and resorts in the west of the Costa del Sol, Almería appears somewhat run-down, but in a way, the air of shabbiness that hangs over everything is what gives the place its appeal. You get the impression that the cracks and crumbling walls conceal layer upon layer of history. The old parts of the city below the Alcazaba, especially around the old Arab quarter, are full of picturesque passages and secret corners. With its countless numbers of bars, Almería also boasts a busy nightlife. The alleys and tiny squares are noisy and lively, teeming with groups of people trawling the tapas bars. Unlike in Granada, the tapas here are mainly seafood-based. The fine art of preparing fried or salted fish, grilled sea snails with garlic, prawns, calamares or mussels has been perfected by the *Almerienses*.

SIGHTS

Alcazaba

★ For its size alone, the Alcazaba of Almería is one of the most impressive fortifications of southern Spain. Dating back to Moorish times, the great citadel enclosed an area of 35 335 sq m and stands 91 m above sea level. Around 20 000 people could fit inside the colossal edifice, which is said to have rivalled the court at Granada in its grandeur. The construction of its triple ring of defensive walls was begun in 955 under the supervision of the city's founder, Abdarrahman III. Successive extensions and reconstructions were carried out by both Muslims and Christians following damage caused by earthquakes and battles. There is a beautiful *garden* behind the first wall, the perfect place for a leisurely stroll. The *watchtower* dates back to the Bourbon King Charles III. Behind the second wall, the remains of former palaces can still be seen. A chapel built in the mudéjar style occupies the site of the former mosque. The third defensive ring was built by the Castilian conquerors; the *Torre del Homenaje* features a late-Gothic portal. The steep climb up the ⬧⬧ *Calle Almanzor* near the Plaza Vieja is rewarded with a fine view over the city, the port, the surrounding countryside, and the beautifully restored defensive structure itself, whose crenellated walls and battlemented towers give it a fairytale appearance.

Summer daily 10.00-14.00 and 16.00-20.00, winter 09.00-13.00 and 15.00-19.00; Entrance: 250 ptas

Almedina (old town)

The *Plaza Vieja* with its fine arcaded façades is a good starting point for exploring the old town. The focal point is the shopping street of *Calle de las Tiendas*; and the *Parque Nicolás Salmerón* on the waterfront with its palms and fountains is a lovely place for a stroll; while the main street, *Paseo de Almería*, has numerous cafés

MARCO POLO SELECTION: ALMERÍA AND THE EAST

1 Alcazaba of Almería
A massive Moorish stronghold perched above the city took centuries to build
(page 54)

2 Almuñecar
This ancient gem lies hidden among the modern construction of the Costa Tropical
(page 58)

and shops. A walk through the Almedina takes you past several churches: the 16th century *Iglesia de Santiago* (*Calle de las Tiendas*) has a magnificent Renaissance façade with the episcopal coat of arms, and an image of a raging saint. Also of interest, and an attractive subject for photos, is the *station*, decorated in ornate Moorish style, just outside the old town on the *Carretera de Ronda*.

Cathedral
This fortified cathedral was built in the 16th century on the foundations of a mosque. The massive structure with its four bulky towers made of square-cut stones was designed to withstand the regular attacks it was subject to by pirates. At one time weapons were deployed here, and even the hexagonal apse has the appearance of a stronghold.
Daily 10.00-12.00 and 17.30-19.30, Plaza Bendicho

RESTAURANTS

Ánfora
Serving Andalusian cuisine at its very best, this is the top restaurant in town.
Daily (except Sun); Calle González Garbín 25; Tel: (950) 23 13 74; Category 1

Bellavista
Fresh fish in delicious sauces, and wonderful desserts. Expensive but worth treating yourself to.
Daily (except Mon and Sun pm); El Aquían; Tel: (950) 29 71 56; Category 1

Club de Mar
Seafood dishes served alfresco on a terrace overlooking the bustling port.
Daily (except Mon); Calle Muelle 1; Tel: (950) 23 50 48; Category 2

SHOPPING

Cuero
Leather goods made in local country farmhouses.
Calle Pedro Jover 26

Madera
Original wooden artefacts, wickerwork and large patchwork quilts (*jarapas*) from the Alpujarras.
Calle Israel 8

Mercasa
An old market hall on the *Circunvalación del Mercado*. Lined with stalls laden with fruit and vegetables, the smell of fresh fish pervades the air. It is a lively and colourful place with a distinctly oriental feel about it.
Mon-Sat 08.00-14.00

ACCOMMODATION

Balneario de Sierra Alhamilla
Wonderful hotel built over a hot spring, situated 20 km inland in the heart of the sun-baked desert landscape.
24 rooms; Pechina; Tel: (950) 31 74 13, Fax: 16 05 27; Category 2

Camping La Garrofa
On the N 340 to Motril, 435 km; Tel: (950) 23 57 70

Country living
For a taste of the rural life, why not rent a country house with family or friends. The *Casa Homos* in Sense in the province of Almería, for example, sleeps four people in two rooms and costs around 35 000 ptas per week. For further information on house rental contact: *RAAR (Red Andaluza de Alojamientos Rurales), Apartado de Correos 2035, 04080 Almería; Tel: (950) 26 50 18 (Spanish and French only), Fax: 27 04 31 (English also).*

SPORT & EXCURSIONS

Diving
Scuba-diving and underwater photography lessons are offered by the *Federación Andaluza de Actividades Subacuáticas (Calle Navarro Rodrigo 26; Tel: 950 24 33 81)* and by *Almerisub (Parque Nicolás Salmerón 11; Tel: 950 26 35 78).*

Excursions
Viajes Koral runs coach tours and trips into the desert region and the Alpujarras mountains that require a certain level of fitness *(Paseo de Almería 47; Tel: 950/25 11 33).*

The *Consultores de Desarrollo Rural* organize an itinerary of guided walks around the local villages *(Calle Sagunto 13; Tel: 950/26 42 40).*

Almerisub organizes excursions into the national desert park of Cabo de Gata, just east of Almería *(Parque Nicolás Salmerón 11; Tel: 950/26 35 78).*

Walks through Andalusia are also organized by *Mundicolor Holidays, 276 Vauxhall Bridge Rd, London, SW1V 1BE; Tel: 0171 828 6021.*

Water sports
Sailing and tennis lessons are offered at the *Club del Mar (Calle Muelle 1; Tel: 950 23 07 80).*

In the neighbouring Roquetas de Mar, the *Club Marítimo Roquetas de Mar (Port Area; Tel: 950 32 29 09)* has a sailing school and facilities for tennis, canoeing and swimming.

ENTERTAINMENT

Almería has around 200 bars concentrated into a very small area – a large number even by Spanish standards. You won't be disappointed by the nightlife, which is always lively. The activity is mainly concentrated in the area between the Paseo de Almería, the Alcazaba and the Parque Nicolás de Salmerón on the waterfront. There's something to suit all tastes and moods here. If you're staying in Almería for the evening, the best place to head for is the *Café Teatro Fennia, Carretera Sierra Alhamilla 324.* If it's clubs and discos you're after, however, you'll need to go further afield to Aguadulce or one of the other coastal resorts.

Oficina de Turismo
Mon-Fri 09.30-14.00 and 16.30-19.00, Sat 08.00-14.00, Parque Nicolás Salmerón; Tel: (950) 27 43 55, Fax: 27 43 60

SURROUNDING AREA

Aguadulce **(L 4)**
This holiday resort west of Almería is the region's attempt to catch up with modern tourism. The hotels and restaurants conform to high standards, and the cleanliness of the sandy beach and quality of the water have earned it the EU's blue flag.

Berja **(K 4)**
It is well worth making a short detour to include this little town (pop. 11 000) on your itinerary. Founded by the Romans, who called it Virgi, it is one of the best places inland to relax and catch a glimpse of daily life. Tucked away

in a valley flanked with vines, the pace of life here is leisurely, and there is an old-world feel about the place. There are a few interesting things to see around town: old houses with traditional Arabic wrought-iron balconies and window grilles, a few vestiges of the old town walls and Arab cisterns. Wander through the ancient streets, enjoy the peace and calm, and soak up the atmosphere.

Cabo de Gata **(M 4-5)**
This desert region east of Almería is the most inhospitable area of the continent and has the lowest annual rainfall anywhere in Europe. The fertile tropical land west of Almería suddenly gives way to a steppe-like landscape characterized by rugged canyons, dried-up river beds, cactuses and agaves, which shimmer in the heat in the shadow of the Sierra Nevada. The road passes by long, desolate, beaches, popular with independent travellers taking

The Wild West in the east: Mini Hollywood near Tabernas

Coastal development has not diminished Almuñecar's charm

refuge from the crowds in the major resorts. This is where the Costa del Sol ends and the Costa Blanca begins. Discovering this solitary, somewhat unexpected side of Spain is one of the pleasures of a holiday in this region. It is the longest stretch of undeveloped coastline on the Spanish Mediterranean. ❧ The view over the Gulf of Almería is breathtaking, especially at night when the harbour stands out as a crescent of lights. Where the road winds its way upwards, the cape lighthouse stands above the steep cliffs, and the ❧ *Mirador de las Sirenas* provides a view over steep precipices and strangely-shaped outcrops. Seals doze on the rocks, flamingos stalk the salt flats, cormorants dip and dive into the sea, and marine life thrives amid a few isolated *fincas* and cactus groves.

Tabernas (L 3)

In the midst of the dusty, barren terrain north of the Sierra de Alhamilla, stands an entire Wild West film set, complete with wooden house and saloon façades – a ghost town left behind by the legendary director Sergio Leone, who filmed *A Fistful of Dollars*, starring Clint Eastwood, here. A number of other westerns have been filmed in this so-called Mini Hollywood, thousands of miles away from the California desert. Cowboy shoot-outs are staged for tourists at weekends. You can even have a drink in the saloon.
Mini Hollywood; Daily 09.00-20.00; Entrance: 595 ptas, children 325 ptas; Calletera de Murcia, 138 km

ALMUÑECAR

(G 5) ★ Almuñecar (pop. 20 000) was founded by the Phoenicians on the foothills of the Sierra de Almijara. The majority of the population here earn their living from the cultivation of exotic fruits grown in hothouses, and from tourism. The climate is consistently hot, providing ideal conditions for the cultivation of sugar cane, avocados, papayas, mangos and medlars.

The ancient town of Almuñecar with its whitewashed houses, winding passages and morning market, still retains much of its original charm, in spite of the building frenzy of recent years. Between the rocky and pebbled stretches, the beaches are sandy. The modern *Marina del Este* is set in a picturesque bay surrounded by cliffs.

SIGHTS

Exploring the town
Sights of interest include the remains of a Roman *aqueduct* with a double row of arches, some ancient *Phoenician tombs*, and the neo-Arabian *Palacete La Najarra* on the Avenida de Europa. The *castle*, built by the Romans, is the town's crowning glory, but it is currently closed to the public for restoration. Climb the ❧ *Peñón del Santo* crag for a fantastic view of the town.

RESTAURANT

Antonio
❁ Good fish dishes, great value for money, popular with the locals.
Bajos del Paseo Marítimo 12; Tel: (958) 63 00 20; Category 2-3

ACCOMMODATION

In Almuñecar itself there are several cheap and cheerful boarding houses and simple *hostales* to choose from.

Camping Herradura
5 km west of Almuñecar in the coastal village of La Herradura.
Paseo Marítimo s/n; Tel: (958) 64 00 56

Camping El Paraíso
This shady, well-maintained site is situated 3 km east of the town. It has its own restaurant and is open all year round.
Tel: (958) 63 23 70

Hotel Salambina
10 km east of Almuñecar, just before Salobreña.
13 rooms; N 340; Tel: (958) 61 00 37, Fax: 61 13 28; Category 3

Hotel Salobreña
A luxury hotel with swimming pool and tennis courts.
130 rooms; N 340; Tel: (958) 61 02 61, Fax: 61 01 01; Category 2-3

INFORMATION

Oficina de Turismo
Paseo Asadillo; Tel: 958/63 11 25

SURROUNDING AREA

Salobreña   (H 5)
This hilltop town by the sea is very popular with the people of Granada, who come here on summer weekends to enjoy the pretty beach and calm surroundings. It is a jumble of whitewashed houses crowned by the remains of a Moorish ❧ castle, and the old town is characterized by narrow alleyways and crooked flights of steps. A nice place to stay is the *Pensión Marí Carmen* which has a lovely ❧ terrace with a view *(24 rooms; Calle Nueva 30; Tel: 958 61 09 06; Category 3)*. The *Mesón El Chaco restaurant (Calle Fábrica Nueva 43; Tel: 958/ 61 12 36; Category 3)* offers good quality at reasonable prices, while *El Peñón (Paseo Marítimo; Tel: 958/ 61 05 38; Category 2)* enjoys a romantic setting.

The heart of the south

The principal city of the Costa del Sol is full of surprises and well worth a visit

The most densely populated region of Andalusia is the heart of the Costa del Sol, centred around the city of Málaga, the second largest in the province after Seville. For decades now, this area has been successfully marketed all over the world as a tourist's paradise and the playground of the rich and famous. After the uncontrolled growth of the boom years, and the rapid decline in standards, the authorities now have tight control over new development. This is particularly noticeable in Málaga, an industrial city and port whose centre gradually became totally run-down, and the sheer weight of traffic virtually brought the city to a standstill. In recent years, however, property developers and local authorities have thankfully begun to instigate reforms, and a great deal of restoration and new building has taken place. The ease and speed with which the historic city centre has been renovated is proof of how much

local officials and businessmen can achieve if they collaborate and implement an official plan of action. Particularly beautiful old squares and buildings, such as the Miguel de Cervantes theatre and the Plaza de la Merced, have been completely overhauled and are now restored to their former glory. Though you may be tempted to bypass the capital of the Costa del Sol, Málaga and its beaches really do merit a closer look.

ANTEQUERA

(**D 2**) ★ The historic city of Antequera (pop. 39 000) lies on a fertile plain *(vega)* in the hills behind Málaga. Founded over a thousand years ago, it boasts two outstanding attractions in its vicinity: a group of megalithic tombs and a fantastic complex of rock formations. The city itself is of interest, with its monumental architecture and intimate squares. The Plaza de San Sebastián is a lovely place to spend some time, sipping a cool drink at one of the cafés or just sitting on one of its stone benches and daydreaming about the past.

Málaga's lush green Paseo del Parque - a haven of peace near the busy port

MARCO POLO SELECTION: MÁLAGA AND THE CENTRAL REGION

1 Antequera
Climb endless flights of steps in one of the most beautiful towns in Spain (page 61)

2 Mijas
Authentically Andalusian despite the tourist hustle and bustle (page 66)

3 Plaza de la Merced in Málaga
Picasso's doves flutter around the most beautiful square in the city (page 69)

4 Nerja
A pretty, lively town in the hills, with an amazing coastal promenade (page 74)

These little squares feed the imagination: history is no longer a textbook subject, but a real and tangible part of the present. The town is spread across several hills, and is full of narrow and winding alleys and flights of stone steps. As you lose yourself in the maze of streets and squares you will be treading the very same ground as Antequera's former conquerors.

SIGHTS

Dolmen Caves

An air of mystery pervades these prehistoric dolmen caves on the eastern edge of the city, which are among the most important megalithic remains on the Iberian peninsula. It is not known who built these burial chambers, nor how the huge stone slabs – some weighing as much as 170 tonnes – were transported down from the mountains. The dolmens are thought to date from around 2500 BC. The most impressive of the caves is the *Cueva de Menga*, which lies under a mound of slate and marl. The 25 m-long passage through the barrow is bordered by 5 monoliths. The 3.2 m-high chamber is covered over with

limestone slabs supported by upright stones; the total weight of the stones is around 1600 tonnes. On one of the side stones you can see some mysterious carvings. The nearby *Cueva de Viera* is made up of 27 interlocking upright stones and is 19 m in length. It is covered by a single, 4 m-long capstone. The burial chambers, now designated national historical monuments, were probably the graves of tribal chieftains who would have been buried together with valuable treasures. It is likely that they were pillaged when the caves were discovered back in 1645. In the grounds of a sugar factory, 4 km away, is the *Cueva del Romeral*, which dates from around 1800 BC. It is similar in its layout to the other two dolmen caves, but its main chamber is crowned by a 4 m-high domed ceiling.
Cueva de Menga and Cueva de Viera: daily (except Mon) 10.00-14.00 and 15.00-17.30; Entrance free; Cueva del Romeral: Tues 16.00-18.00, Weds-Sat 09.30-14.30 and 16.15-18.30, Sun 10.00-14.00; Entrance free

Old town

The old town of Antequera has been classified as a historical monument, and contains a number of interesting sacred and secular buildings. Of particular note are the two churches of *Real Colegiata Santa María la Mayor* (Plaza Santa María), a huge Renaissance building, and *El Carmen*, with its pretty *artesonado* (*mudéjar*-style) carved wooden ceiling; both date from the 16th century. Antequera has a total of 25 churches and monasteries still inhabited by enclosed orders of monks and nuns. The stately *Arco de los Gigantes* (Calle de Pastillas), the 'Giants' Arch', built in 1585, features the coat of arms of Antequera. The remains of the Moorish *castle* lie within a park dominated by the ✧ *Torre de Papabellotas*, an angular bell tower from the top of which you can gaze down over the rooftops, and the *Peña de Los Enamorados* – the Lovers' Peak. According to legend, the daughter of a wealthy Moor and her Christian lover, fleeing an angry mob, threw themselves off the crag and plummeted to their deaths.

RESTAURANTS

La Espuela
Andalusian food by the bullring.
Daily (except Sun); Plaza de Toros; Tel: (95) 270 26 76/30; Category 2

Parador de Antequera
The restaurant in the Parador is the best in town.
Paseo García del Olmo s/n; Tel: (95) 284 02 61; Category 2

HOTELS

Parador de Antequera
A middle-ranking establishment with restaurant, swimming pool, and a beautiful garden.
55 rooms; Paseo García del Olmo s/n; Tel: (95) 284 02 61, Fax: 284 13 12; Category 2

La Sierra
A modern hotel with facilities for the disabled.
30 rooms; N 331, 134 km; Tel: (95) 284 54 10, Fax: 284 52 65; Category 2-3

La Yedra
Simple accommodation in a good location with a good-value cafeteria.
15 rooms; N 331; Tel: (95) 284 22 87; Category 2-3

INFORMATION

Oficina de Turismo
Mon-Fri 10.00-13.00 and 16.00-18.00; Plaza de San Sebastián 7; Tel: (95) 270 25 05, Fax: 270 39 32

SURROUNDING AREA

Garganta del Chorro   (C 2)
This impressive limestone gorge is a natural wonder. It rises up as high as 400 m on either side of the Río Guadalhorce that rushes through it. Look out for the ✧ *Camino del Rey* (King's Way). This is a narrow concrete catwalk which clings to one of the steep faces and runs the full length of the gorge. Although it offers stunning views, you should only venture out if you have a good head for heights, and steady nerves. Sections of it are in a fairly advanced state of disrepair, and rockfalls are not infrequent. If you are feeling adventurous, however, it's an exciting walk with amazing views.
On the C 337, 50 km north of Málaga

El Torcal (D 2)

This national park 16 km south of Antequera is laced with numerous walking trails (marked out with arrows), of varying lengths, that wend their way through a labyrinth of huge limestone rocks. It is spread across a plateau that lies between 1000 m and 1300 m above sea level and covers around 20 sq km. The limestone has been constantly pounded by wind and rain, and over the centuries this erosion has resulted in some amazing rock formations, turning the slopes of the Sierra Pelada into a surreal landscape with a marvellous array of naturally-formed causeways, passages, bridges, and sink-holes. The limestone plateau is also the natural habitat of a variety of birds of prey.

FUENGIROLA

(D 4) Known as Suel to the Romans, Fuengirola (pop. 43 000) is actually of Phoenician origin. It is situated at the entrance to a tropical valley, where sugar cane and custard apple trees are cultivated in the shade of the Sierra de Mijas. The most striking feature of this town is the seafront with its long promenade and excellent sandy beach, which has won an EU blue flag for its cleanliness and good facilities. The nicest part of Fuengirola is the area around the *puerto*, where sleek modern boats are anchored alongside old fishing vessels. In summer, crowds of tourists stroll along the ✪ ♣ Paseo Marítimo and through the old town district of Casco Viejo.

SIGHTS

Castillo Sohail

✍ This ruined castle was built in the 18th century over the foundations of a 10th-century Moorish fortress.

Parque Zoológico

The only zoo on the Costa del Sol keeps 500 different animals.
In summer Mon-Fri 10.00-14.00 and 17.00-21.00, in winter 09.00-13.00 and 15.00-19.00, Sat and Sun 10.00-21.00; Calle Camilo José Cela

The strange and impressive limestone landscape of El Torcal

RESTAURANTS

La Langosta
The oldest restaurant in town. Lobster is a speciality.
Evenings only, closed Sun; Calle Francisco Cano 1; Tel: (95) 247 50 49; Category 1-2

La Mirage
❧ Dine to the accompaniment of live music and entertainment. Great view from the terrace.
Evenings only, closed Sun; N 340, 215 km, Carvajal; Tel: (95) 221 18 03; Category 1

The Shakespeare
✪ A generous buffet on Sundays, live music on Mondays, dinner-dance on Saturdays. This restaurant has been an institution for more than twenty years.
Calle Juan Sebastián Elcano; Tel: (95) 247 36 42; Category 2

SHOPPING

The *Mercadillo de los Martes* (every Tuesday) is a market with a truly Arabic feel. The *Centro Comercial Las Rampas* has a huge selection of postcards with witty captions in different languages. *Nicholson Jewellers (Calle Marbella)* specializes in silver.

HOTELS

Byblos Andaluz
A modern hotel with crèche.
144 rooms; Urbanización Mijas Golf, P.O. Box 138; Tel: (95) 246 02 50, Fax: 247 67 83; Category 1

Florida
A well-maintained, medium-sized hotel at mid-range prices.
116 rooms; Paseo Marítimo s/n; Tel:
(95) 247 61 00, Fax: 258 15 29; Category 2-3

Yamasol
Reasonably priced with facilities for the disabled.
84 rooms; Avenida Ramón y Cajal 35; Tel: (95) 246 17 47, Fax: 258 43 00; Category 3

SPORT & LEISURE

Club Náutico de Fuengirola
Facilities for all kinds of water sports.
Tel: (95) 247 04 06

Parque Acuático Mijas
A relatively new leisure centre in Mijas-Costa. Various swimming pools with several giant slides. Especially suited to families, as there are excellent facilities for children. If you find the restaurant a bit expensive you can always bring your own picnic.
April/May 10.30-17.30, June 10.00-18.00, July/Aug 10.00-19.00, Sept 10.00-18.00; N 340, 209 km; Bus service from Fuengirola bus terminal

Patronato Municipal de Deportes
The municipal *Elola Sports Centre, Tel: (95) 246 67 77* offers aerobics, fencing, gym and karate sessions at reasonable prices.

ENTERTAINMENT

A variety of exhibitions, concerts, plays and other events are regularly staged at the ✪ *Casa de la Cultura, Calle Estación Córdoba; Tel: (95) 247 90 00*. There is an underground ♣ *disco (Calle Martínez Catena s/n)* or you can go to the *Fortuna Night Club* which stages a variety show every night featuring Spanish ballet and Flamenco.

There is also a *casino (daily 20.30-04.00; Entrance: from 3500 ptas)*. Most of the *cinemas* are in the streets of *Arroyo, Francisco Cano, Tejada* and *Vertedor*.

INFORMATION

Oficina de Turismo
Parque de España; Tel: (95) 246 74 57, Fax: 246 51 00; Mon-Fri 09.00-14.00 and 16.00-19.00, in summer 17.00-20.00, Sat 10.00-13.00.

SURROUNDING AREA

Mijas (D 4)
★ ◆ Eight km north of Fuengirola, perched on a hillside is one of the most beautiful little inland villages (pop. 6000) in the Costa del Sol. Mass tourism has not left Mijas unscathed, but if you can ignore the crowds of tourists snapping up 'genuine local artefacts', the pungent smells of the *burro* (donkey) taxis, their persistent drivers, and the overpriced souvenir shops, you will discover something of the 'real' Andalusia in the picturesque narrow cobbled streets, wrought-iron balconies, terracotta and marble façades, and clusters of pine trees.

First settled around 2600 years ago, there is evidence of Mijas' historic past around every corner: in the *Plaza de la Constitución*, in the *parish church* of La Muralla with its *mudéjar* architectural features, and in the *Casa Consistorial* (town hall), which also houses the *Tourist Office (Plaza Virgen de la Peña; Tel: (95) 248 59 00)*. The *Carromato de Max* museum has a bizarre collection of miniature items, such as Leonardo da Vinci's *Last Supper* on a grain of rice, the head of Winston Churchill carved out of a piece of chalk, a naval battle depicted on the head of a drawing pin, even some dissected fleas.

The view from the ◆ *Mirador de Mijas* of the villas and houses jumbled together on the slopes below is wonderful. Up here you will also find a ◆ *shrine* to the patron saint of the village, La Virgen Santa María de la Peña, set in a grotto. The altar is overflowing with passport photos, cheap jewellery, hair bands, and locks of hair, all placed there as offerings to the saint.

If you visit Mijas on a Sunday during the bullfighting season (and, of course, if you are not against bullfighting), you could go to a corrida in the small *Plaza de Toros*, the only square bullring in Spain *(Tel: (95) 248 52 48)*.

The *Artesanías Granada (Plaza Virgen de la Peña s/n)* with its beautiful vases, ceramics and stitched leather bags is a cut above most of the cheap souvenir shops here. There are rows of cafés and snack bars around the *Plaza de la Constitución. El Capricho*, a rustic inn with lovely views over the centre of Mijas, is a good place for a down-to-earth meal *(closed Weds; Calle de los Caños 5; Tel: (95) 248 51 11; Category 3)*, while the *Valparaíso* just outside the village serves haute cuisine *(evgs only, closed Sun; Carretera Mijas-Fuengirola, 4 km; Tel: (95) 248 59 75, Fax: 248 59 96; Category 1)*. The *Mesón de la Fuente* at the entrance to the village serves huge steaks from the grill and *boquerones en vinagre* (anchovies pickled in vinegar) at tables on a cosy terrace *(closed Mon; Avenida México 1; Tel: (95) 248 58*

91; Category 2-3). The village hotels are nothing to write home about. You will find better accommodation in the surrounding countryside.

MÁLAGA

(D 3) The city landscape is dominated by the castle of Gibralfaro and the Alcazaba. The medieval citadel was once a perfect vantage point from which to keep a look out for invaders. Today, in place of the pirate ships, you can watch the cargo ships as they approach the busy port. During the Spanish Civil War, Málaga was fiercely disputed and the city was badly damaged by sustained bombardment. 43 churches and monasteries were burned down in 1931 alone (the year of the proclamation of the Republic) and by 1937, when Málaga finally fell to the Fascists, the whole of the inner city was destroyed and lay in ruins. Commerce, the port and tourism are now Málaga's main sources of income, while Spaniards flock to Andalusia's second-largest city (pop. 535000) to go shopping. Founded by the Phoenicians, transformed into a port by the Romans, and endowed with architectural treasures by the Arabs, this city on the Río Guadalmedina is truly the economic heart of the Costa del Sol.

SIGHTS

Alcazaba

This 11th-century Moorish fortress, built on an elongated mound, was once the seat of the Nasrid rulers. During the 1930s it was lavishly restored. The three concentric walls conceal offset entrance gates, small ornamental gardens adorned with water features, and graceful semicircular arches. The palace, which features some fine stucco work and ceiling decorations, now houses the archaeological museum.
Fortress: daily 09.30-13.30 and 17.00-20.00 or 16.00-19.00 in winter; Entrance: 25 ptas; Museum: Mon-Sat

A quiet whitewashed street in the ever popular hillside village of Mijas

The Alcazaba dominates Málaga and affords a wonderful view of the city

10.00-13.00 and 17.00-20.00, in winter 10.00-13.00 and 14.00-19.00; Entrance: 250 ptas

Cathedral

Málaga's cathedral is affectionately known as *La Manquita*, 'the one-armed lady', because it only has one tower (the west tower was never finished). In all it took 250 years (1528-1783) to build. Construction was delayed time and again due to lack of funds and arguments over details. The cathedral's most impressive features are the west and north portals (the latter reached through a courtyard of orange trees), and the vast, majestic interior, which is 117 m long and 72 m wide. The vaulted ceiling rises up from sturdy Corinthian columns. Several grand masters of Spanish ecclesiastical architecture, including Alonso Cano, contributed to its construction. The west front, however, remains incomplete.
Daily 10.00-13.00 hrs and 16.00-17.30 hrs; Plaza de la Catedral; Entrance: 200 ptas

Gibralfaro

◁▷ Above the Alcazaba is the Gibralfaro castle. The funds set aside for its restoration were evidently not sufficient to carry out even the most basic improvements, but it's well worth the strenuous climb just to see the imposing view over the city. The panorama from the castle encompasses the harbour and sea, the town hall and bullring, the historical old town, the chequered high-rise conglomeration to the west, and the villas and pretty apartment complexes to the south. With a good pair of binoculars you can even watch the *toreros* practising their manoeuvres in the bullring. It is satisfying to observe that no high-rise building in the city rises above the cathedral tower.
Bus route 35 from Paseo del Parque

Paseo del Parque

❖ The park near the port with its rich subtropical vegetation is the pride of the *malagueños*, and with good reason. Both the park and the palm-lined Paseo were laid out around the turn of the century as part of a comprehensive town planning programme. On public holidays families parade their children in their Sunday best, while old men and couples of all ages sit on the numerous benches and watch the world go by. You can take a ride around the area in a horse-drawn carriage, but make sure you settle on the price beforehand. The rides usually last 20 to 30 minutes.

Plaza de la Merced

★ ☻ ♣ This is the most beautiful square in the city, and is still populated with the doves which featured so strongly in the early works of Picasso. The city's most famous son was born very close to the Plaza de la Merced. The paved square with its lovely old pavilions, enclosed by wrought, iron railings, is lined with houses which have all been renovated in recent years. It has been a central meeting place for the townspeople for generations.

Teatro Romano

The discovery of the Roman amphitheatre near the Alcazaba, on the site of the palace that housed the city's cultural centre, was the cause of a bitter dispute for many years. It was immediately proposed that the *Casa de la Cultura* should be demolished in order to uncover the *Teatro Romano*, restore it and use it for large-scale open-air theatre productions. Many people, however, were dead against the idea of destroying the Cultural Centre. The battle which ensued was bitterly fought by both sides; and in 1995 it was finally decided to sacrifice the cultural centre. Standing in this semicircular amphitheatre it is incredible to think that on this very spot, more than 2000 years ago, people were making observations on their life and times through speech and song.

Casa Natal Pablo Picasso

At the end of the 1980s, a trust fund was set up for the upkeep of the birthplace of the city's greatest son. Pablo Picasso was born in Málaga on 25 October 1881. Thousands of books on the life and work of the painter, videos, posters, and other memorabilia; everything, indeed, which has ever been said or written about Picasso is gathered together here. The rooms are filled with documents on the various artistic phases of the master. A number of desks for art historians are set out here, giving the place a studious atmosphere.

Mon-Sat 09.00-14.00 and 17.00-20.00; Plaza de la Merced 15; Entrance free

Museo de Bellas Artes

The Museum of Fine Arts is housed in the Buena Vista Palace, an austere Renaissance building dating from the 1540s. It is currently closed, however, while it is

The ornamental gardens of the Alcazaba are a fine example of Moorish irrigation expertise

being transformed into a Picasso Museum to house 138 works bequeathed to the Andalusian regional government by one of the artist's daughters-in-law.
Expected to reopen in 1998 or 1999

RESTAURANTS, CAFÉS & TAPAS BARS

Antonio Martín
◁◁▷ This traditional restaurant, established in 1886, is a good place to sample *fritura malagueña,* the fried fish for which Málaga is so renowned, while enjoying the sea view.
Daily (except Sun pm); Paseo Marítimo 4, La Malagueta; Tel: (95) 222 21 13; Category 1-2

La Cancela
❂ A cosy, atmospheric restaurant, rustic in style and very popular with the locals. The Andalusian menu includes some excellent fish soups.
Daily (except Weds); Calle Denis Belgrano 3; Tel: (95) 222 31 25; Category 2

Casa Vicente
❂ This old-fashioned fish restaurant, decked out with plastic furniture and tucked away in a narrow street off the Alameda Principal, is a Malagueño favourite.
Calle Comisario 2; Tel: (95) 222 53 97; Category 2-3

Chinitas
Offers an extensive fish menu and outdoor dining in summer.
Calle Moreno Monroy 4; Tel: (95) 221 09 72; Category 3

El Corte Inglés
❂ An abundant buffet is laid out in the cafeteria of this large department store. Help yourself to anything you like and pay at the till when you leave.
Mon-Sat until 20.30; Avenida de Andalucía 4-6; Category 2-3

Gibralfaro
A smart café with a good selection of tapas and a wide range of sweets and desserts.
Daily (except Sun); Pasaje Chinitas

Lo Güeño
❂ ♣ Tasty tapas in a wonderful atmosphere. The locals come here to get in the mood for the evening's entertainment.
Calle Martín García 11; Tel: (95) 222 30 48; Category 2

El Jardín Cafetería
A bar with an air of sophistication: a candelabra-topped piano and grandfather clock stand beneath a gilded mirror; ceiling fans turn lazily above; the bar itself is luxuriously long. In warmer weather the activity spills outside on to the stepped passage.
Calle Cañón 1; Category 2

Orellana
❂ ♣ A well known and popular tapas bar with many *malagueños* among its clientele.
Calle Moreno Monroy 3; Tel: (95) 222 30 12; Category 2-3

Rincón de Mata
The long bar on the ground floor is a place of pilgrimage for tapas-lovers; the restaurant on the first floor serves original fish dishes.
Calle Esparteros 8; Tel: (95) 222 31 35; Category 2

Café-Bar Santander
Simply furnished, excellent tapas.
Daily (except Sun); Calle Granada 36

La Solera

Huge wooden barrels dominate the room, from which the best Spanish wines and sherries are poured.
Calle Reding 10; Tel: (95) 260 20 24; Category 2

La Tasca

✪ A nice little place with a carved wooden bar, where you can pick at morsels of Serrano ham to whet your appetite. It can be a bit of a struggle to get to it through the afternoon and early evening crowds.
Calle Martín García 12; Category 3

SHOPPING

Carrera

Jeans and casual fashions.
Calle Nueva 8

Club de Gourmet

The food hall on the sixth floor of the El Corte Inglés department store stocks a wide range of goods.
Avenida de Andalucía 4-6

Cosmopolis

A deli with well-stocked shelves, great cheeses, and many varieties of tinned fish and wines.
Calle Marqués de Larios 2

Flea market

Stamps, old coins, pictures, photographs and postcards. A treasure trove for numismatists.
Sun morning; Plaza de la Constitución

Galería de Arte

Gallery in a centrally-located old town house which exhibits works by contemporary Spanish painters. Exhibitions change monthly.
Calle Nino de Guevara 2

Grabados Somera

The much-acclaimed master craftsman Pedro Somera Abad works on his skilful engravings of traditional scenes, views of the city and animals in this tiny workshop in a narrow alley in the old town. He sells his pieces at reasonable prices.
Calle Correo Viejo 7

Mercado Central

Large, slightly run-down market hall selling fresh local Andalusian fruit and veg, meat and fish. An interesting feature of the neo-*mudéjar* style building is the huge 13th-century horseshoe arch which forms the entrance. It is decorated with two coats of arms and the Islamic inscription 'Only Allah is the victor'.
Mon-Sat 08.00-15.00; Calle Atarazanas 8

Zara

A boutique in the pedestrian area that's popular with trendy young Spaniards. You can often pick up some real bargains here.
Calle Liborio García 6

ACCOMMODATION

Avenida

Central and cheap.
Alameda Principal 5; Tel: (95) 221 77 29; Category 3

Camping Balneario del Carmen

This campsite (640 pitches) on the coast road is open all year. It may not be blessed with the most idyllic location, but it does have well maintained facilities. It has a tennis court, and the beach is near by. Just outside the site is a supermarket where you can stock up on all the basics.

Avenida Pintor Sorolla 26 (bus route 11 from Paseo del Parque); Tel: (95) 229 00 21

Chinitas
Hostel on the second floor of a slighty tatty-looking house, conveniently located in a pedestrian area right in the heart of the city.
14 rooms; Pasaje Chinitas 2; Tel: (95) 221 46 83; Category 3

Don Curro
Three-star establishment just outside the town centre. A good base for exploring the city.
105 rooms; Calle Sancha de Lara 7-9; Tel: (95) 222 72 00, Fax: 221 59 46; Category 2

Las Vegas
Convenient hotel on the outskirts of the city. 34 new rooms in the annex all have sea views.
106 rooms; Paseo de Sancha 22; Tel: (95) 221 77 12, Fax: 222 48 89; Category 2

Los Naranjos
Hotel just outside the city centre. Typical Andalusian decor. Underground car park.
41 rooms; Paseo de Sancha 35; Tel: (95) 222 43 16, Fax: 222 59 75; Category 2

Málaga Palacio
❧ Málaga's top hotel, with swimming pool on the roof terrace, and panoramic views.
225 rooms; Cortina del Muelle 1; Tel/Fax: (95) 221 51 85; Category 1

Parador de Málaga Gibralfaro
❧ Renovated hotel near the Moorish fortress. Romantics will enjoy the sunsets and views of the sea glistening in the twilight from the terrace or the swimming pool. Nearby golf course offers both golf and tennis coaching.
38 rooms; Monte Gibralfaro; Tel: (95) 222 19 03, Fax: 222 19 04; Category 1-2

Parador de Málaga del Golf
On the edge of the city, surrounded by the greens and fairways of a golf course. Beautifully fitted out in traditional Andalusian style.
60 rooms; Apartado de Correos 324; Tel: (95) 238 12 55, Fax: 238 21 41; Category 1

Pensión Rosa
Simple boarding house right in the city centre.
26 rooms; Calle Martínez 10; Tel: (95) 221 27 16; Category 3

Youth Hostel (Albergue de la Juventud)
For international YHA members only. The dormitories sleep four.
Plaza Pio XII 6 (final stop on bus route 18); Tel: (95) 230 85 00, Fax: 230 85 04; Category 3

SPORT & LEISURE

Beaches
Málaga has over 15 beaches within its boundaries, the best of which are the *Pedregalejo, El Palo* and ❧ *La Malagueta.*

Caving
Excursions to the region's caves are organized by the *Federación Andaluza de Espeleología (Plaza Picasso, 29640 Málaga; Tel: (95) 258 13 27).*

Golf
The *Lauro Golf Los Caracolillos (Alhaurín de la Torre; Tel: (95) 241 27 67)* is an 18-hole golf course set in

lovely surroundings. Information on courses throughout the province can be obtained from the *Federación de Golf de Andalucía (Paseo del Pintor Sorolla 34; Tel: (95) 222 55 90)*.

Riding

The *Centro Ecuestre Artecus (Apartado 94, Alhaurín de la Torre; Tel: (95) 241 28 18)* organizes short and long (up to several days) horse-riding treks through peaceful, unspoilt countryside.

Sailing

For information on the various sailing opportunities on offer contact the *Federación de Vela (Calle Sagasta 2; Tel: (95) 222 55 00)*.

SPANISH COURSES

A Spanish course is the ideal way to get to know the country and the locals. The *Malaca Instituto* and its *Club Hispánico* student halls offer double-room accommodation and are a 15-minute bus ride from Málaga's city centre *(Cerrado de Calderón, Calle Cortada 6, 29018 Málaga; Tel: (95) 229 32 42, Fax: 229 63 16)*. The courses run during the summer holidays are mostly attended by young people (aged 16-25). The wide-ranging choice of tuition courses includes a standard language course of 20 hours per week and individual lessons with 6 hours' tuition per day; older students are welcome. The 'courses for the active older person' are a recent innovation. Participants not only learn to roll their 'r's, but they can also try their hand at flamenco, join an aerobics class, have massage sessions and learn how to cook typical Andalusian dishes. Courses at the *Malaca Instituto* can be booked through various language tour operators; prices for two weeks half board range from 74 800 to 147 000 ptas.

ENTERTAINMENT

Antigua Casa de Guardia

Ancient *bodega* established in 1840 where wine is poured straight from the barrel. Customers stand at the bar or at small tables to sample the local produce – there are more than 20 red wines to choose from, which you can accompany with seafood *tapas*.
Two entrances: Alameda Principal 18, Calle Pastora 6

Calle Beatas

✪ ☆ This little street leading off the Calle Granada draws young locals like a magnet. The pubs and disco-bars are heaving, especially at weekends. It is a great place to meet *malagueños*.

El Pimpi

✪ ☆ One of the most original bars in Málaga. It offers plenty of space in a succession of small rooms whose ceilings are decorated with ivy. Frequented by artists and young people.
Calle Granada 62

Salsa

☆ Salsa and mambo are played in this bar all night. Excellent lively atmosphere.
Calle Méndez Núñez 1

Teatro Cervantes

This theatre housed in a listed palace, restored in 1987, offers a varied programme of opera, dance and music festivals, and avant-garde theatre productions.

Plaza del Teatro; for information Tel: (95) 222 02 37, bookings 222 41 00; Tickets: 1500 to 2500 ptas

INFORMATION

Oficina de Turismo
Mon-Fri 09.00-19.00, Sat 10.00-19.00, Sun 10.00-14.00; Pasaje de Chinitas 4; Tel: (95) 221 34 45, Fax: 222 94 21

SHARED TRAVEL & ACCOMMODATION BUREAU

Iberstop sets up cheap car-share arrangements. A shared journey from Málaga to Barcelona, for example, costs around 5500 ptas. Longer-distance journeys can also be arranged. In order to ensure the safety of the passengers, the car registration details and personal information about the drivers are investigated and recorded, and the roadworthiness of the vehicles is also checked. This organization can also find you cheap private rooms in Málaga and the Costa del Sol.
Iberstop, Calle María 13/2, 29013 Málaga; Tel: (95) 225 45 84

SURROUNDING AREA

Jardín Botánico-Histórico La Concepción   **(D 3)**
With its trees up to 150 years old, water features, and beautifully-planted pathways, this botanical garden is food for the soul.
Open 09.30 - 19.00; Carretera de la Pedrizas on the outskirts of the city, reached from the N331.

El Retiro bird sanctuary   **(D 3)**
The El Retiro *finca* in Churriana, 10 km west of Málaga, was founded by a bishop in 1669 and has recently been reopened following renovation. Under the supervision of a German ornithologist, the park with its woods, aviaries, and little waterfalls, has gradually been transformed into a home for thousands of varieties of birds from all over the world.
Daily 09.00-18.00; reached via the N 340; Entrance: 1000 ptas, children 650 ptas

NERJA

(F 3) ★ The local authorities have been careful to prevent unscrupulous developers from throwing up high-rise hotel blocks that would ruin the picturesque streets and mar the sea views of this pretty little town (pop. 14000). With its small-scale hotels and relaxed atmosphere, Nerja has managed to preserve something of its old-fashioned charm. The beaches here are part sand, part shingle, and are subdivided by rocky outcrops into picturesque bays and inlets, connected by a promenade that winds its way along the seafront below the town. Although it does attract quite a few tourists, you can usually find a quiet corner here, and both the beaches and the water are clean.

SIGHTS

Balcón de Europa
🌿 ☀ A magnificent promenade built on a rocky outcrop with a wonderful view stretching out to sea between two lovely bays. Its tropical palms and masses of colourful flowers, along with the restaurants and cafés that run along its length,

make it a very pleasant place to spend some time and meet the locals. The ruins of a fortress and two iron cannons are reminders of the past.

Cuevas de Nerja

These limestone caves just outside the town stretch for 800 m and extend to a height of 60 m. There are a number of impressive stalactites and stalagmites which are imaginatively lit, and the cave paintings, with images of dolphins, are thought to date back 20 000 years. The excellent acoustics of these immense caverns are also put to commercial use when classical concerts, and even ballet productions, are staged every July in this spectacular natural setting.

May-mid Sept daily 09.30-21.00, all other times 10.00-13.30 and 16.00-19.00; Entrance: 500 ptas

RESTAURANTS

Almijara

A reasonably-priced family restaurant with a spacious garden terrace and barbecue.
Daily (except Mon); Residencial Verano Azul 41-42; Tel: (95) 252 59 79; Category 2

La Cocina

In addition to full English breakfasts and regional specialities, vegetarian food is also served here. You order at the bar, then cross the passage on to the flower-filled terrace hung with cages that house brightly-painted wooden birds. Barbecues are set up on the terrace on summer evenings.
Calle Cristo 10; Tel: (95) 252 03 87; Category 2-3

The Gallery

✪ ✗ Very British, with its popular and cheap *Super Sunday Lunch* (*Sun 12.00-15.00*). Attracts young Brits and locals alike.
Daily (except Mon); Calle Los Huertos 74; Tel: (95) 252 07 58; Category 2

Udo Heimer

If you fancy a change from tapas and fried fish, why not try Udo Heimer's spicy Hamburg goulash, or a plate of rolled beef with red cabbage and boiled potatoes. The German chef has won several accolades from the Spanish authorities, as well as the prestigious American 'Golden Cook Award for World Best Restaurants'. Reservations essential.
Daily (except Mon); Pueblo Andaluz 27; Tel: (95) 252 00 32; Category 1

SHOPPING

Carmari (Calle Pintada 34) is an unashamedly kitsch souvenir shop complete with pink façade and a hoard of knick-knacks. The *Casa del Arte (Calle Cristo 13)* sells a range of arts, crafts, and paintings. Ángela Minguez, the proprietress of *Gaia (Calle Cristo 18)*, loves to explain to her customers, in Spanish or English and with much gesticulating, how she makes her glass pieces. She also sells clothes, bags and jewellery, all of which are handmade.

HOTELS

Balcón de Europa

↘↗ A hotel in the old town, renowned for its location and its cuisine.
105 rooms; Paseo Balcón de Europa 1; Tel: (95) 252 08 00, Fax: 252 44 90; Category 2

Casa Maro

☃☃ Only three minutes from Nerja by car, in the direction of Almuñecar, this small hostel with its pretty balconies and beautiful terrace is also very cheap.

24 rooms; N 340, Maro; Tel: (95) 252 95 52; Category 3

Villa Flamenca

A modern, well-appointed Andalusian-style hotel in the *Urbanización Nueva Nerja*. It has a swimming pool and inner courtyard, and is just 250 m from the beach.

88 rooms; Calle Andalucía 1; Tel: (95) 252 18 69, Fax: 252 21 96; Category 2

Bar 23 Bar

❖ ☃ A great bar with whitewashed walls, lots of wood, Mexican beer, sangria and, of course, a selection of tapas. It is full every evening. A small inner courtyard provides a welcome breath of fresh air for non-smokers.

Calle Pintada 23

Oficina de Turismo

Puerta del Mar 2, 29780 Nerja; Tel: (95) 252 15 31

Frigiliana   (F 3)

This pretty little hilltop village (pop. 2400), perched at a height of 433 m between Nerja and the Sierra de Almijara, was the site of some important finds of human bones and pottery dating back to between 3000 and 1700 BC. Remains of a Phoenician necropolis as well as evidence of Roman occupation, not to mention the huge Moorish inheritance, show that settlers have been drawn to the region for thousands of years, largely because of the pleasant climate. Although there is now little evidence left of the town's

The caves of Nerja: the most unusual concert hall in Spain

ancient past, Frigiliana is nevertheless worth singling out because of the well-preserved *mudéjar*-style centre. A wonderful far-reaching view out to sea and over the mountains can be enjoyed by fortunate guests at the *Hotel Las Chinas (14 rooms; Plaza Capitán Cortés 14; Tel: (95) 253 30 73; Category 3)*.

Torre de Mar/Vélez-Málaga (E 3)
Torre de Mar, to the east of Málaga, is the resort district of the town of Vélez-Málaga (pop. 54 000) which lies a little further inland. This former Phoenician settlement sits on a hill in the fertile valley of the river Vélez. The old town with its crooked passages is remarkably intact. The most noteworthy among its historic buildings are the magnificent 17th-century *Palacio de los Marqueses de Beniel*, the aisled *church of Santa María la Mayor* built in the *mudéjar* style, and the 18th century *fountain of Fernando VI*. The skyline is dominated by the imposing watchtowers of the Moorish stronghold, parts of whose defensive walls are still standing. In contrast to the historic old town, Torre de Mar is a fairly unremarkable modern resort, full of high-rise hotel blocks. It is a typical *urbanización* – functional but rather soulless. The long shingle beach only has basic facilities, but it does have the advantage of plenty of space. Every morning, the fishing harbour is the scene of noisy fish auctions.

The *Caravaning Laguna Playa* is a reasonable campsite; follow the signs from the N 340 beyond the town *(Tel: (95) 254 06 31, Fax: 254 04 84)*.

TORREMOLINOS

(D 4) With its 90 pubs, 40 discos, 80 fish restaurants and numerous nightclubs, Torremolinos (pop. 35 000) is not the place to come if you want to experience Andalusian tradition. This huge *urbanización* is entirely geared towards catering for the needs of international tourism. The fine sandy beach, numerous beach bars and sports clubs may not be the ideal location for those in search of peace, relaxation and a spot of culture, but Torremolinos could be considered as a good base for interesting and educational excursions in the area. Until just a few decades ago, the busiest and brashest resort on the Costa del Sol was nothing more than a fishing hamlet made up of just 15 houses. The seeds of its meteoric rise were sown in 1932 a few kilometres further west in Montemar, where the visionary entrepreneur Carlotta Alessandri bought a piece of the hilly countryside. When asked what plants she intended to cultivate on the barren land, the bold woman retorted 'tourists', and went on to enthuse about the 'Spanish Riviera' and its many attractions. During the confusion surrounding the Spanish Civil War the project lay dormant, but the foundations had been laid. After World War II the business tycoon Marqués de Nájera built himself a summer villa in Torremolinos, and wealthy families, members of the aristocracy, and all kinds of eccentrics followed him to the land of continual sunshine. The artistic community, made up mainly of film stars and writers, was the next to arrive.

Torremolinos, the 'tower of the mills' (some of the old mills can still be seen in the district of Pimentel) soon became a hedonists' playground, increasingly populated with all kinds of social climbers. The fishermen and watermill owners were completely overrun by the pleasure-seekers, though they did profit substantially from the Northern European obsession with sun, sea and sand.

SIGHTS

San Miguel
The city centre is made up of the pedestrianized San Miguel area, together with the *Plaza Costa del Sol* and its surrounding streets. At the seaward end of the long Calle San Miguel stands a 14th-century Moorish tower. From here the *Cuesta del Tajo* leads past the *Molino la Bóveda*, a 16th-century mill, and down to the *Playa Bajondillo*, considered by many to be the best beach in Torremolinos. A rocky outcrop divides this beach from the equally popular *Playa Carihuela*.

RESTAURANTS

Europa
Excellent traditional Andalusian food at reasonable prices, situated a little way out of town on the road to Cádiz.
Vía Imperial, Montemar; Tel: (95) 238 80 22; Category 3

Frutos
Superb cuisine, mostly based on fresh fish.
Daily (except Sun); Urbanización Los Álamos; Tel: (95) 238 14 50; Category 1

Beach restaurants
The following restaurants *(all Category 2-3)* on the *Playa Carihuela*, the former fishing village promenade (reached via the road which branches off near the Hotel Las Palomas), are all recommended for their traditional seafood cuisine. Try the *pescaíto frito*, small fish fried in olive oil, which is a particular speciality of this district, washed down with a glass of chilled dry sherry.
Guaquín, Calle Carmen 37, Tel: (95) 238 45 30
El Roqueo, Calle Carmen 35, Tel: (95) 238 49 46
La Jábega, Calle Mar 17, Tel: (95) 238 63 75
La Marina, Paseo Marítimo, Tel: (95) 238 93 71

SHOPPING

The pedestrianized *Calle San Miguel* is a good place for shopping, window-shopping, eating ice cream, drinking coffee, and watching the world go by. Prices here tend to be lower than in Marbella. Fresh produce is sold at the morning *market (Calle Periodista Antonio Saenz 16)*, while gifts and expensive jewellery and watches can be found at *Ideal (Calle San Miguel 38)*. If you have met the love of your life on the beach and want to have his or her name imprinted on your person forever, you can have it done by a professional at *Templo Tattoos (Plaza de Gamba Alegre)*.

ACCOMMODATION

Beatriz
A small hostel on the beach with balcony views over the Playa de Bajondillo.

8 rooms; Calle Peligro 4; Tel: (95) 238 51 10; Category 3

Camping Torremolinos

Conveniently located campsite on the edge of the city, just below the road to Málaga, with a small supermarket and cafeteria. The main drawback is that it is quite a way from the beaches. Open all year round.
Tel: (95) 238 26 02

Guadalupe

Boarding house with sea views; some rooms have a balcony. The in-house restaurant is nice and cheap.
8 rooms; Calle Peligro 13; Tel: (95) 238 19 37; Category 3

Parador del Golf

Swimming pool, library, tennis courts and golf course.
60 rooms; Carretera de Málaga, Churriana; Tel: (95) 238 12 55, Fax: 238 21 41; Category 1

Youth Hostel
(Albergue de la Juventud)

Youth hostel in an old, white-washed building with veranda. Central and close to the beach. The dormitories sleep four. Shower facilities.
Closed Sept-May; Avenida Carlotta Alessandri 127; Tel: (95) 238 08 82; Category 3

SPORT & LEISURE

There are facilities for golf, tennis, minigolf and many water sports. The *Aquapark Torremolinos* with its giant water slides and performing dolphins is a great place to take the kids (*May-Sept daily 10.00-20.00; Carretera de Circunvalación s/n; Entrance: 2000 ptas, children 1500 ptas*).

ENTERTAINMENT

Most of the ☘ clubs and discos are concentrated around the Plaza Costa del Sol. They don't really get going until midnight, and in summer dancing continues well into the morning.

INFORMATION

Oficina de Turismo

Mon-Fri 08.00-15.00, Sat 09.00-14.00; Urbanización La Nogalera, Calle Guetaria, local 517, 29620 Torremolinos; Tel/Fax: (95) 238 15 78

SURROUNDING AREA

Alhaurín el Grande (C 4)

This peaceful picturesque village on the edge of the Sierra de Mijas is only 20 km inland from the holiday resorts but is altogether a different world. Alongside the ubiquitous Moorish castle ruins there is a parish church with the adjacent grotto of the *Ermita de la Virgen de la Pena*. The village has the added attraction of the first 18-hole children's golf course in the world. A round at the *Alhaurín Golf & Country Club* costs 1800 ptas.

Benalmádena Aquarium (D 4)

This spectacular, huge underwater aquarium in Puerto Marina reveals the hidden world of sharks, eels, starfish and sea anemones. This was the first underwater theme park in Spain. Inaugurated in 1995, it is one of the most up to date of its kind in the world.
Daily 10.00-18.00; Parque Submarino Puerto Marina, Calle Fernando González Moreno; Entrance: 950 ptas, children (age 4-12) 650 ptas

Paradise regained

*Where the Mediterranean jet-set
and traditional rural lifestyles co-exist*

At the height of the tourist boom, this former high-society Eldorado risked permanent ruin by the worst excesses of mass tourism. Thankfully, the resorts are undergoing a gradual regeneration and their old Andalusian charm is creeping back in. Although there is still no other stretch of coastline in Europe with such a high concentration of luxury hotels and golf courses, this picturesque district is no longer the exclusive domain of the rich and famous who once patrolled the streets and bays in their stretch limousines, luxury yachts and designer clothes. The 'beautiful people' and the paparazzi have been largely replaced by tourists wanting to see more of the Andalusian way of life.

ESTEPONA

(**B 4-5**) Estepona is full of southern charm, with its whitewashed houses, pantiled roofs, balconies

The most luxurious yachts in the world are moored in the marinas in and around Marbella

overflowing with flowers, and street names painted on colourful ceramic tiles. Lemon cultivation was for a long time the main source of income here, but this has been largely superseded by tropical fruit. Both the architecture and atmosphere of the town reflect a harmonious blend of Moorish and Christian cultures.

SIGHTS

Old town

The old town of Estepona is typically Andalusian in style with its narrow cobbled streets, winding passages, and jumble of pretty whitewashed houses. The *parish church* dates back to the 15th century while, in the *Calle Castillo*, remains of the Moorish *castle walls* can still be seen. The main meeting place is the ✪ ✦ *Plaza de las Flores*, strewn with the chairs and tables laid out by local cafés.

RESTAURANTS

Bacchus Bistro

✪ Light, but wholesome food at reasonable prices. The Sunday buffet is popular with locals.

MARCO POLO SELECTION: MARBELLA AND THE WEST

1 Plaza de los Naranjos in Marbella
The 'square of the orange trees' – where all and sundry meet for a stroll and a chat (page 84)

2 Benahavis
A picturesque mountain village with a harmonious architectural blend of old and new, and an unusual gallery (page 83)

Mon-Sat evgs only, Sun lunch only; Calle Bermúdez; Tel: (95) 279 57 97; Category 2

La Casa de mi Abuela
Charcoal-grilled steaks and Argentinian wine.
July/Aug, evgs only; Calle Caridad 54; Tel: (95) 279 19 67; Category 2

Mesón Cordobés
A traditional tapas bar.
Daily (except Sat); Plaza de las Flores 16; Category 3

SHOPPING

Flea market
Every Sun, *09.00-15.00* in the *Puerto Estepona*; jewellery, antiques, leather goods and crafts.

HOTELS

Buenavista
Simple, but well located.
38 rooms; Paseo Marítimo; Tel: (95) 280 01 37; Category 3

El Paraíso
If variety is the spice of life, this hotel is well seasoned: Japanese gardens, a swimming pool complex, the largest heated indoor pool on the Costa del Sol, saunas, fitness gyms, tennis courts, and a golf course created by the US champion Gary Player.
188 rooms; N 340, 167 km; Tel: (95) 288 43 17, Fax: 288 20 19; Category 1

Stakis Paraíso
Modern hotel with swimming pool and golf course.
200 rooms; N 340, 167 km; Tel: (95) 288 30 00, Fax: 288 20 19; Category 2

SPORT & LEISURE

Excursions
Daily trips conducted by *A Taste of Spain (Tel: (95) 288 65 90; 7000 ptas incl. lunch)*: Mon and Tues into the mountains, Weds and Fri into the white villages, and Thurs to the Spanish Riding School in Jerez de la Frontera.

Health Centre
In the *Centro de Medicina Tradicional China*, connected to the El Paraíso hotel, clients are pummelled by masseuses, and various programmes are offered under medical supervision for slimming, giving up smoking, regaining energy, etc. The only centre for Chinese medicine in Spain. A massage and acupuncture session costs around 7000 ptas.

N 340, 167 km; Tel: (95) 288 30
00, Fax: 288 20 19

Naturism

If you want to strip off completely,
there is a nudist colony just 3 km
from Estepona. It has several
swimming pools, sports facilities,
holiday homes and shops.
*Urbanización Costa Natura; N 340,
157 km; Tel: (95) 280 15 00*

INFORMATION

Oficina de Turismo

*Mon-Fri 09.30-13.30 hrs and 17.00-
19.00, Sat 10.00-13.00; Paseo Marítimo Pedro Manrique s/n; Tel: (95)
280 09 13, Fax: 279 21 81*

SURROUNDING AREA

Benahavis   (B 4)

★ Wandering through the narrow streets and across the squares
of this lovely mountain village
(pop. 1200) you will come across
some modern apartment blocks
among the more traditional
houses. Surprisingly, a harmony
has been struck between the old
and new throughout the village.
La Aldea, the gallery of David
Marshall, an Englishman who has
lived in Andalusia for many years,
promotes design. The large exhibits of steel, sheet metal, and
other bulky materials are highly
original. The extensive gallery
occupying several rooms on the
Plaza de la Iglesia is well worth
a visit *(Mon-Fri 11.00-14.00 and
17.00-21.00, Sat 17.00-21.00).* After
you've perused the gallery, you
can go for dinner at the ✪ *El
Fogón* restaurant, also on the
square *(evgs only, closed Mon; Tel:
95/285 51 90; Category 1-2).* Or
you can try the *Aquarium (Avenida

de Andalucía; Tel: 95/285 52 67;
Category 3)* which boasts a lovely
terrace.

Tarifa   (A 6)

A must for surfers and wind-
surfers. The most southerly point
of Europe, it is constantly wind-
lashed and the water is as hard as
steel – the perfect conditions for
the skilled acrobats who can
power through the waves on
their boards at over 30 mph. This
is the spot where two powerful
wind systems meet: the Levanter
which blows in from the east and
the Poniente that drives in from
the west to the Ensenada de
Valdevaqueros at the tip of the
bay, where most of the surfers
congregate. Courses are available
for beginners and advanced
surfers alike and cost upwards of
3500 ptas. Enquire at the *Spin out
Surfbase/Fanatic Fun Center (N 340,
76 km; Tel: 956/23 63 52),* the
*Club Mistral (Hurricane Hotel; Tel:
956/68 49 19),* or the *Surfcenter
Dos Mares (Hotel Dos Mares; Tel:
956/68 40 35).* Inexpensive meals
can be enjoyed in the *La Nueva
Urta restaurant (Daily from 20.00;
Plaza Juan de Austria; Tel: 956/68
06 69; Category 3),* while Spanish
food is served in the little *Mesón
la Albariba* in a passage in the
old town *(Closed Sun; Calle San
Francisco 6; Category 2).* Accommodation is available at the trendy
*Surferhotel 100% Fun (12 rooms, 4
apartments; N 340, 76 km; Tel/Fax:
956/68 00 13; Category 2)* or in the
simple old town hotel of *La Mi-
randa (12 rooms; Calle San Sebastián
48; Tel: 956/68 44 27, Fax: 68 11
62; Category 3).* Those in the know
will confirm that the nightlife is
even more tiring than the waves.
La Ruina (Calle Santa Trinidad 9),

on the town walls, is the focal point, while the *Café Central (Calle Ucho el Bravo)* is where the hardened nocturnals go for breakfast. Information from the *Patronato local de Turismo, Daily 10.00-14.00; Paseo Alameda; Tel/Fax: (956) 68 09 93.*

MARBELLA

(**C 4**) Marbella (pop. 84 000) is both a sophisticated modern enclave of glass, reinforced concrete and glamour, yet still maintains a strong traditional side, visible in the historic centre. To fully appreciate this town, you need to see both sides. The marble-paved promenade is where the rich and famous can be seen strolling between the marina with its bobbing yachts and the old lighthouse. The *Plaza de los Naranjos*, on the other hand, has been the focal point of the ordinary townsfolk for centuries. Groups of young people hang out on the square alongside the older generations who come here to gossip and catch up on the news. Couples peer into boutiques while young children play noisily in the nearby streets. In terms of style and quality of life, Marbella is definitely top of the concrete resort league.

SIGHTS

Old town

The oldest part of the resort is set away from the sea on a hill. Its narrow streets and squares are a combination of Christian and Moorish styles, and it is only exceeded in its Andalusian charm by Mijas. The *Rincón de la Virgen*, where the streets of Remedios and Dolores meet, is adorned with colourful flowers. The Rococo portal of the 16th-century *Iglesia Mayor de la Encarnación* at the end of the Calle de Carmen opens on to a romantic church square which is dominated by the tower of a 9th-century Moorish palace. The *San Francisco monastery* and the *Hospital San Juan de Dios* are both Renaissance.

Plaza de los Naranjos

★ The octagonal *marble fountain* is Renaissance, the *pilgrimage chapel* is 15th century and the *town hall* and the *Casa del Corregidor* (Chief Magistrate's House) date back to the 16th century. The interior of the town hall is decorated with pretty frescos and panelling.

Promenade la Alameda

This promenade is lined with trees, many of which are centuries old, including some particularly magnificent pines and gum trees. The ceramic-tiled benches are wonderful.

MUSEUM

Bonsai Museum

One of the largest European Bonsai tree collections is laid out in a modern park which also features some rare examples of the wild olive tree.
Daily 11.00-13.30 and 17.00-21.00; Parque Arroyo de la Represa; Entrance: 400 ptas, children 200 ptas

RESTAURANTS

La Belle Époque

Small restaurant in the old town. Spanish and international cuisine. *Daily (except Sun); Calle Ortiz de Molinillo 14; Tel: (95) 277 84 45; Category 2*

La Fonda

One of the best restaurants in Spain. The top quality menu combines aspects of traditional and international cuisine with culinary refinement. The atmospheric inner courtyard is the most popular place to dine. Early booking is essential.

Daily (except Sun); Plaza Santo Cristo 10; Tel: (95) 277 25 12; Category 1-2

Plaza

❖ Cheap, yet serves the best paella in town.

Plaza General Chinchilla 6; Tel: (95) 277 11 11; Category 3

Plaza Epoca Café Bar

❖ An Art Nouveau tapas bar, always full of locals.

Closed Mon; Plaza Ramón Martínez 1; Tel: (95) 282 81 42; Category 3

Santiago

A fish restaurant right by the sea. Sophia Loren and Michael Jackson, among others, have graced its tables, but the majority of the clientele are Spanish. Specialities are *boquerones fritos* (fried anchovies) and *mero en salsa* (grilled grouper). The wine cellar boasts 120 000 bottles.

Paseo Marítimo 5; Tel: (95) 277 00 78; Category 1

SHOPPING

Antiques

There is a well-stocked junk shop in the narrow *Calle Valdés 6*. Enjoy a rummage among old pistols and door knockers, steam irons and cameras, jugs, cutlery, and worn religious objects. An *antique and flea market* is held every Saturday morning in *Puerto Banús* near the bullring.

Leather

One of the best leather and shoe shops on the whole of the Costa de Sol is *Bravo* in the *Avenida Ramón y Cajal 5*. El Caballo stocks everything for the serious rider. *Avenida Ricardo Soriano*

Menswear

Top-quality classic suits at reasonable prices can be found at *Massimo Dutti (Avenida Ricardo Soriano)* on the *Plaza Marqués de Salamanca*. You can be clothed from head to toe here from 40 000 ptas.

ACCOMMODATION

Alfil

One of the few cheap places to stay in Marbella. Great for those on a tight budget.

40 rooms; Avenida Ricardo Soriano 19; Tel: (95) 277 23 50, Fax: 277 29 58; Category 2

Camping-Caravaning Marbella Playa

Campsite between the road and the sea, shaded by trees, with swimming pool and hot showers. *N 340, 192.9 km; Tel: (95) 283 39 98, Fax: 283 39 99*

Coral Beach

A luxury hotel between the main road and the beach. Tennis, golf and health club.

170 rooms; N 340, 176 km; Tel: (95) 282 45 00, Fax: 282 62 57; Category 1

La Estrella

A small boarding house on the coast road. Not very peaceful, but a practical choice for anyone just passing through.

15 rooms; Calle San Cristóbal 36; Tel: (95) 277 94 72; Category 2-3

Golf fanatics are spoilt for choice

Puente Romano
26 luxuriously appointed, three-storey buildings, all specially designed to face the sun, surrounded by palms, a subtropical garden, streams and waterfalls, hidden ponds, and swimming pools. This amazing hotel complex is considered to be 'One of the Leading Hotels of the World'.
219 rooms; N 340 177 km; PO Box 204; Tel: (95) 277 01 00, Fax: 277 57 66; Category 1

Pyr Marbella
Stay where the jet set stay – but at half the cost.
319 rooms; Puerto Banús, Avenida Principal s/n; Tel: (95) 281 73 53, Fax: 281 79 07; Category 1-2

Youth Hostel
(Albergue Juvenil de Marbella)
A youth hostel in the upper part of town, just 2 km from the beach, with nice reception hall, and swimming pool in the park. A total of 111 beds in 5- and 6-bed dormitories. From 900 ptas per person per night.
Trapiche 2; Tel: (95) 277 14 91, Fax: 286 32 27

SPORT & LEISURE

Balloon flights
Sunset flights over Ronda and the rugged coast, with champagne and tapas.
Aviación del Sol; Tel: (95) 287 71 49; from 20 000 ptas

Boat hire
Club Marítimo de Marbella (*Puerto Deportivo José; Tel: (95) 277 57 00; Banús*); Marina Marbella (*Tel: (95) 281 55 97*); and Seacrest (*Tel: (95) 278 60 00*).

Golf
The favourable climate guarantees that golfing passions can be

indulged all year round. A huge variety of golf courses. Prices range from 2500 to 9500 ptas.

Mountain biking
Whole and half-day tours in guided groups from 1600 ptas.
Mountainbike Aventura, Pueblo Platero 8, bloque 1; Tel/Fax: (95) 283 12 04

Riding
Centro Ecuestre Club del Sol organizes treks (one-day or longer) through the mountainous region inland *(Sitio de Calahonda; Tel: (95) 283 81 24)*. The riding school *Los Montros* behind the *Río Real golf course (N 340, 183 km; Tel: (95/277 06 75)* offers 45-minute riding lessons for 2000 ptas; horses can also be hired from 3000 ptas for one-and-a-half hours.

Sailing
Two hours exploring the coast in the capable hands of a seasoned skipper.
Super Bonanza; daily departures from 12.00 from Puerto Banús; Tel: (95) 238 55 00

Water sports
The *Beach Club* at the *Puente Romano hotel* offers all water sports facilities *(Apr-Oct daily 11.00-18.00; N 340, 177 km)*. Mundo Mágico offers underwater rides in miniature submarines *(Apr-Oct; Puerto Banús; Tel: (95) 281 85 00 and 281 70 20; 4000 ptas, children 2000 ptas)*.

ENTERTAINMENT

Bar Cascada
Spacious, sophisticated lounge bar in the *Puente Romano* hotel. Piano music.
Daily 19.30-00.30, N 340, 177 km

Casino Nueva Andalucía
Eight American and four French roulette tables, blackjack, punto y banca, and baccarat, with a restaurant and swimming pool to boot.
Daily in winter 20.00-04.00, in summer 21.00-05.00; Hotel Andalucía Plaza, N 340, 226 km; Tel: (95) 291 40 00

INFORMATION

Oficina de Turismo
Mon-Fri 09.00-14.00 and 16.00-19.00, Sat 10.00-13.00; Glorieta de la Fontanilla; Tel: (95) 277 14 41, Fax: 277 94 57

SURROUNDING AREA

San Pedro de Alcántara   (B-C 4)
This small town (pop. 20 000) is well worth considering as an alternative to Marbella. Once an agricultural centre, San Pedro has in recent years opened up to tourism, and the newly modernized *puerto deportivo* should entice even greater numbers of tourists. A short way out of town, on the *Río Verde*, lie the ruins of the Roman settlement of *Silniana*, which was destroyed in 356 by a seaquake. The Lakeview is a riding school where you can either take lessons (2000 ptas per hour) or hire a horse (2500 ptas) for a beach ride *(Guadalmina Alta; Tel: (95) 278 69 34)*.

Yachting marinas   (C 4)
The marinas around here are the most famous on the Mediterranean. The biggest and most luxurious yachts in the world moor up at *Puerto Banús*, 6 km from Marbella. The latest marina to be built is the ultra-modern *Cabo Pino*, 17 km east of Marbella.

Practical information

Important addresses and useful information
for your visit to the Costa del Sol

ANGLING

The Costa del Sol countryside has many rivers and reservoirs rich in fish. A rod licence (*permiso de pesca*) is required, obtainable from the *Jefatura Provincial del ICONA, Licencia Nacional de Caza y Pesca, Jorge Juan 39, Madrid; Tel: (91) 225 59 85*, or from the local municipal ICONA office.

BANKS

Opening hours: Mon-Fri 08.30-14.00. The maximum amount you can cash a Eurocheque for (the best exchange rate) is 25 000 ptas. Cash machines are available in ever-increasing numbers.

BUSES & TRAINS

Here, in the congested south of Spain, public transport can often be a good alternative to hire cars, so long as there is a convenient service available. Buses run frequently in all the towns, and there is a good network between all the main tourist attractions. There is a useful frequent rail connection between Málaga and Fuengirola.

CAMPING

The Costa del Sol and Granada are sadly lacking in campsites. The few that do exist are not usually equipped with the best of facilities, although attempts have been made recently to improve the situation. Camping rough isn't strictly forbidden in many areas, but it is frowned upon; anyone pitching their tent too near a main road or in a dry river bed should expect to be cautioned.

CAR HIRE

All the main international car hire firms have branches at the airports, in cities, and in the larger resorts. Depending on the category of vehicle, hire charges range from 4000 to 10 000 ptas, with VAT, fully comprehensive insurance and additional mileage on top. Some tour operators offer fly/drive packages, which are often the cheapest option. The minimum age is 21 and drivers must have held a full licence for at least a year. The cars are not always in the best of condition; as a rule, the cheapest operators tend to provide the worst-maintained vehicles.

CONSULATES & EMBASSIES

Consulates in Southern Spain
British:
Plaza Nueva 8, Sevilla;
Tel: (95) 422 88 75

Edificio Duquesa, Calle Duquesa de
Parcent 8, Málaga
Tel: (95) 221 75 71

American:
Paseo Delicias 7, Sevilla;
Tel: (95) 423 1885

Visitors from Australia, Canada
and Ireland will need to contact
their embassy in Madrid.

Spanish embassies
in Britain:
39 Chesham Place, London SW1 8SB;
Tel: 0171 235 5555

in the USA:
2375 Pennsylvania Avenue NW,
Washington DC 20037;
Tel: 452 0100/728 2340

in Ireland:
17a Merlyn Park, Ballsbridge,
Dublin 4; Tel: (01) 269 1640

CREDIT CARDS

The usual cards are accepted in
most of the large hotels, restaurants and shops, and for car hire.

CUSTOMS

Although customs restrictions
have been lifted for goods im-
ported between EU countries
since 1993 (provided they are for
personal use) certain recommended limits apply: 800 cigar-
ettes, 400 cigarillos, 200 cigars,
90 l wine (of which max. 60 l

sparkling), 20 l liqueur, 10 l spirits
per person (over 17 years of age).

DOCTORS

Medical care in Granada and on
the Costa del Sol is generally very
good; inland medical care is often
provided by emergency centres
(*casa de socorro*). For minor complaints it is often easiest to consult
the local pharmacist (*farmacia*)
anywhere you see a green cross.
Otherwise the local police station
(emergency number 091) will be
able to tell you where the nearest
doctor (*médico*) can be found. EU
citizens should obtain an E 1-11
form (available from post offices)
prior to departure, entitling them
to free treatment in public hos-
pitals and with most State-
approved doctors. An additional
means of identification should
also be presented.

DRIVING

You'll need a valid driving licence,
log book, country identification
sticker, and green insurance card;
a bail bond is recommended.
Speed limits: in built-up areas 50
km/h; on main roads 90 km/h;
motorways 120 km/h. Motorway
toll fees are around 15 ptas/km.
A telephone information service
on road and traffic conditions is
available for tourists in French
and English: *Tel: (901) 30 06 00*
(Mon-Fri 08.00-18.00, Sat and Sun
08.00-16.00).

DRUGS

Although the Spanish may have a
more relaxed attitude to cannabis,
any drug use is strictly forbidden.
Any requests by local people to

Road Rage

Anyone racing past the otherwise friendly Andalusians in a fast car will earn themselves some disapproving looks. Driving aggressively behind someone or cutting them up when overtaking will provoke at the very least irritation, if not a high-speed chase or other aggressive reaction. It is advisable to drive extra carefully and courteously. The same applies to pedestrians: be extra vigilant when crossing the road. Zebra crossings do exist in Andalusia, but they are not taken that seriously. You may have to wait some time before a car stops and they may even swerve around you as you are crossing one. Andalusian roads have in recent years been greatly improved, but there are still plenty of narrow, steep and winding lanes, especially in the mountains, where a degree of caution should be exercised.

take bags, packages or the like out of the country with you should be flatly refused. The *Caldería Nueva* with its pubs and tea rooms is one of Granada's most beautiful little streets, but it is also a popular haunt among drug dealers who can be extremely pushy and should always be answered with a firm *'absoluto no'*.

ELECTRICITY

This is usually 220 V AC; 125 V sockets are now quite rare. A continental adaptor is essential for British users.

EMERGENCY TELEPHONE NUMBERS

To reach the police *(policia)* and emergency services *(ambulancia)*, dial 091, or 080 for the fire brigade *(bomberos)*.

HOTELS

The prices of hotels have been gradually increasing over recent years, but generally remain good value for money; only the luxury range of hotels are positively expensive. The prices fixed to the inside of the hotel room doors are binding. All complaints should be addressed to the local tourist offices.

INFORMATION

Spanish National Tourist Office (SNTO)
in Britain:
57-58 St James's Street, London SW1A 1LD; Tel: 0171 499 0901 or 0171 499 1169

in the USA:
666 Fifth Avenue, New York, NY 10103; Tel: (212) 265 8822

Addresses for the local information centres are given in the relevant sections of this guide.

NEWSPAPERS

All the main international newspapers, weekly magazines and periodicals are readily available in Granada, Málaga and other larger towns and resorts, and often even in smaller places, on the day after publication. Spanish-speaking visitors will get the best information from the national newspaper *El País*.

NUDISM & TOPLESS BATHING

Going topless is not a problem, but complete nudism will not be tolerated on public beaches. However, the Costa del Sol does provide three of the small number of Spanish nudist beaches: they are near Almería, Almuñecar and Estepona.

OPENING TIMES

Most of the shops are open from 09.00 or 10.00 until 13.00 or 14.00 and again from 16.00 or 17.00 until 20.00 or 20.30, and on Saturdays mornings only. In Andalusia, however, these opening times are not rigidly adhered to, and in the main tourist centres department stores and supermarkets are often open all day, including at weekends. Petrol stations that are centrally-located tend not to observe the siesta, but most others will.

PASSPORTS

Since 1 January 1993, border restrictions have been lifted within the EU, although travellers from EU countries will still need to carry a valid passport or identity card. Children under 16 years of age must be entered on their parents' passport or possess their own. American and Canadian visitors do not need a visa to enter Spain, but Australian nationals will need to apply for a visa from the Spanish consulate.

POST & TELEPHONES

Post offices (*Correos*) are generally open Mon-Sat from 09.00-13.00, and the main post offices open again in the afternoon from 17.00-19.00. Stamps *(sellos)* can also be bought in hotels and *tabac* bars. International calls made from Telefónica offices are much cheaper than in any hotel. They usually stay open until well into the evening and calls are up to 25% cheaper after 22.00. You will also find plenty of telephone kiosks where you can dial abroad direct, but you will need a pile of change or a phone card (*tarjeta de teléfono*). These come in units of 1000 and 2000 ptas and are available from tobacconists. The minimum charge for a telephone call abroad is 300 ptas.

To make an international call first dial 07, wait for the continuous tone, then dial the country code (UK: 44; Ireland: 353, USA and Canada: 1), followed by the

The gitanos on the Sacromonte

Granada's *gitanos* stage regular performances of guitar music and flamenco dancing for tourists, most of which are held on the hill of Sacromonte where the majority of them live. The cost of these gypsy shows is often excessive. Prices of drinks can be extortionate – you even have to pay to take photos. So, if you do decide to try one out, be prepared to be ripped off. You should also avoid this area altogether after dark, unless you go with a pre-arranged group.

Almería has countless bars and restaurants to choose from

area code and subscriber number omitting the initial 0. When phoning Andalusia from abroad, the international country code for Spain is 34, which should be followed by the local area code omitting the initial 9.

TIPS

Taxi drivers, waiters and hotel staff will generally expect 5-10% as a tip, while porters, attendants, hairdressers, shoe cleaners, etc. should be tipped at your own discretion.

WHEN TO GO

The Costa del Sol is a good place to visit all year round, as the weather is always mild. Even in December you can expect an average of five hours' sunshine a day, and the braver members of the community see in the new year by swimming in the sea at a temperature of 16°. High season lasts from the end of April to the middle of October; during this period the prices increase everywhere. In Granada and inland

In the Marco Polo Spirit

Marco Polo was the first true world traveller. He travelled with peaceful intentions forging links between the East and the West. His aim was to discover the world, and explore different cultures and environments without changing or disrupting them. He is an excellent role model for the 20th-century traveller. Wherever we travel we should show respect for other peoples and the natural world.

WWF

from the Costa del Sol it can turn very cold, but temperatures rarely fall below zero except in the Sierra Nevada, which is guaranteed snow from December to April. In high summer it can also get exceedingly hot inland.

YOUTH HOSTELS

Not all Spanish youth hostels are open all year round. Rates currently range between 1400 and 2500 ptas per person per night. Full details of addresses, opening times and general conditions can be obtained from YHA offices either in England or in Spain: *YHA, Trevelyan House, 8 St Stephen's Hill, St Albans, Herts AL1* or *Alianza Cristiana de Jóvenes* (YMCA), *Salustiano Olozaga 12, izq., Madrid; Tel: (91) 431 59 85,* or *Red Española de Albergues Juveniles, Calle Ortega y Gasset 71, 28006 Madrid; Tel: (91) 347 77 00.*

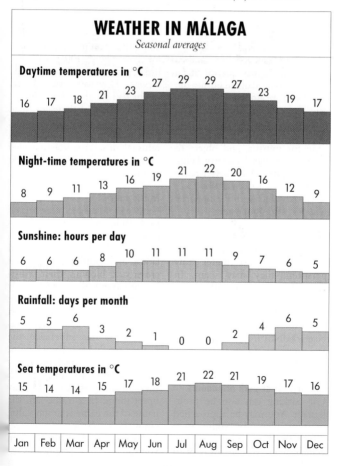

WEATHER IN MÁLAGA
Seasonal averages

Daytime temperatures in °C

16 17 18 21 23 27 29 29 27 23 19 17

Night-time temperatures in °C

8 9 11 13 16 19 21 22 20 16 12 9

Sunshine: hours per day

6 6 6 8 10 11 11 11 9 7 6 5

Rainfall: days per month

5 5 6 3 2 1 0 0 2 4 6 5

Sea temperatures in °C

15 14 14 15 17 18 21 22 21 19 17 16

| Jan | Feb | Mar | Apr | May | Jun | Jul | Aug | Sep | Oct | Nov | Dec |

Do's and don'ts

*How to avoid some of the traps and pitfalls
that face the unwary traveller*

The Barrio de la Chanca in Almería

The climb up to the *Alcazaba* through the gypsy quarter of *La Chanca* is to be avoided during the day if you are alone and by everyone, alone or not, after dark. The poverty-stricken people living there in slum conditions have no time for tourists, and object to their 'photogenic' poverty being photographed. A far better route is the access road via the *Calle Almanzor* near the Plaza Vieja, which is also signposted.

Beggars

It's best to avoid getting involved with beggars, no matter how persistent they may seem. In Spain, begging is a much more serious business than elsewhere. Demands can exceed more than just a few loose coins, and some beggars do turn aggressive if they feel you have not been generous enough.

Self-styled car park attendants

Car parking can also be problematic. You may be approached in some places by young men offering to keep an eye on your vehicle while you are away or to help guide you into a tight space for *'veinte duros'* (100 ptas) – the usual price for this unsolicited service. However irritated you might feel it's always best to just agree as many of these so-called 'car park attendants' are running protection rackets, and if you refuse their services you may well find your car vandalized when you return to it.

Traffic police

Granada's police are often armed to the hilt, and are world champions when it comes to whistle-blowing. The smartly-uniformed ladies and gentlemen stand at crossroads, blowing their whistles and frantically waving their arms in an attempt to tame the never-ending stream of traffic. This display of Latin temperament does not supersede the normal traffic laws. Panicking or setting off in too much of a hurry in an attempt to comply with their manic gesturing will only upset them. In a traffic jam the name of the game is to stay calm, enjoy the acrobatic performances and seize the opportunity when you can to gain a little headway.

INDEX

*This index lists all the places, sights and museums mentioned in this guide.
(G) = Granada, (M) = Málaga. Bold numbers indicate the main entry in the
case of multiple references, italics indicate photos.*

What do you get for your money?

 Spanish notes come in denominations of 1000, 2000, 5000 and 10000 ptas and there are coins to the value of 1, 5, 10, 25, 50, 100, 200 and 500 pesetas (ptas). Most major credit cards are widely accepted, even at filling stations; Eurocheques (up to a maximum of 25000 ptas) on the other hand are not always recognized in shops and restaurants. You'll find cash machines in all the larger towns and cities where you can withdraw money using credit cards and Eurocheque cards (don't forget your pin number).

Here are a few prices to give you some idea of what your money is worth: the cost of a basic breakfast ranges between 300 and 600 ptas, while for lunch or dinner you should expect to pay at least 3000 ptas. A mineral water costs 100 ptas, a glass of orange juice, beer or wine 150 to 175 ptas; tapas start at 150 ptas. Self-caterers will find the best value at supermarkets, especially given current favourable exchange rates. The same is true for shops and bou-

tiques, but it is always advisable to shop around; Marbella, for example, is around one third more expensive than Torremolinos. The conversion table below is based on the current tourist rate (Sept 1997).

£	Ptas	Ptas	£
0.50	117	100	0.43
1.00	235	200	0.85
2.00	469	300	1.28
2.50	586	400	1.71
3.00	704	500	2.13
4.00	938	750	3.20
5.00	1,173	1000	4.26
7.50	1,759	1500	6.40
10.00	2,345	2000	8.53
15.00	3,518	3000	12.79
20.00	4,690	4000	17.06
25.00	5,863	5000	21.32
30.00	7,035	7500	31.98
35.00	8,208	10000	42.64
40.00	9,380	12500	53.30
45.00	10,553	15000	63.97
50.00	11,725	17500	74.63
75.00	17,588	20000	85.29
100.00	23,450	25000	106.61
250.00	58,625	50000	213.22
500.00	117,250	100000	426.44